2/11

$34.95
B/REAGAN
Ronald Reagan : 100 years

RONALD REAGAN

100 YEARS

RONALD REAGAN
100 YEARS

Ronald Reagan Presidential Foundation

Foreword by Senator Howard H. Baker, Jr.

HARPER
DESIGN

An Imprint of HarperCollins Publishers

B
REAGAN

HarperCollins books may be purchased for educational,
business, or sales promotional use. For information please write:
Special Markets Department, HarperCollins*Publishers*,
10 East 53rd Street, New York, NY 10022.

First published in 2010 by
Harper Design
An Imprint of HarperCollins*Publishers*
10 East 53rd Street
New York, NY 10022
Tel: (212) 207-7000
Fax: (212) 207-7654
harperdesign@harpercollins.com
www.harpercollins.com

Distributed throughout the world by
HarperCollins*Publishers*
10 East 53rd Street
New York, NY 10022
Fax: (212) 207-7654

Library of Congress Control Number: 2010937796
ISBN: 978-0-06-201486-3

Design by Agnieszka Stachowicz

Printed in the United States
First Printing, 2010

CONTENTS

A Word from Frederick J. Ryan, Jr., Chairman of the Ronald Reagan Presidential Foundation

WERE HE HERE TO CELEBRATE HIS 100TH BIRTHDAY, RONALD REAGAN might be a little embarrassed by all the fuss for what he would likely refer to as "the sixty-first anniversary of my thirty-ninth birthday." It's a pretty safe bet, however, that he would enjoy the parties—not because they were about him, but because he and Nancy would be with family and friends. And he would definitely have a big piece of chocolate cake.

No doubt he would be excited about, and impressed by, how much our country and the world have changed since his arrival on the scene a century ago. William Howard Taft was president in 1911 when his thirteenth successor was born in a small apartment above a bank in Tampico, Illinois. Back then there were no such things as the Internet, flat screen televisions, penicillin, electric cars, or space travel, to cite just a few examples.

Over time things always change, of course, but much of what is different—and better—about America and the world today is because of Ronald Reagan. His years in the White House changed the course of history forever. The Reagan presidency restored America's strength and position in the world, enabling freedom to triumph, eventually resulting in the collapse of the Soviet Union. At home, a sick economy was made well, unleashing America's entrepreneurial and innovative spirit and leading to some of the most important and transforming discoveries and inventions in the history of mankind.

Ronald Reagan would probably not be as surprised at how much things have changed as one might think. That's because he had an abiding faith in the American people, and believed there was nothing they could not do. To him, there were no limits.

If, somehow, he could be asked what he thought of the mind-boggling advances made during the past 100 years, chances are he would say, "Well, what did you expect? After all, we're Americans."

In celebrating the centennial of Ronald Reagan's birth, we remember an extraordinary man who touched our hearts. A man whose natural optimism gave us hope. Whose strong principles and devotion to the cause of freedom gave us confidence. Whose smooth, reassuring voice gave us courage. And whose unwavering belief in the American dream made us believe in ourselves.

He is missed, but his spirit lives on through the foundation he established to continue his legacy, and through the millions of people around the globe who live—and will live—in freedom.

The pictures and words in this book tell Ronald Reagan's uniquely American story. He was the embodiment of what is possible here. It never ceased to amaze him that a boy from such humble beginnings could achieve such great dreams. Yet even when he was at the very pinnacle of power, he never forgot who he was and from where he had come. That's probably what we liked best and miss most about him.

Fred. Ryan

Foreword by
Senator Howard H. Baker, Jr.

"HOWARD BAKER . . . TOLD ME ON THE STEPS OF THE CAPITOL, AT THE TIME OF THE INAUGURAL, 'MR. PRESIDENT, I WANT YOU TO KNOW I WILL BE WITH YOU THROUGH THICK.' AND I SAID, 'WHAT ABOUT THIN?' AND HE SAID, 'WELCOME TO WASHINGTON.'" —RONALD REAGAN

Ronald Reagan's political career began in the same year—1966—that I was first elected to the United States Senate from Tennessee. He became governor of California and launched a political movement that fourteen years later would catapult him to Washington and the White House as the fortieth president of the United States.

Years later, our paths crossed again on the political landscape. In 1976, when he challenged President Gerald Ford for the Republican nomination, my wife, Joy, and I invited the Reagans to be our guests at our home in Huntsville, Tennessee. It was a social visit and a night of "Southern hospitality." He was campaigning in my home state, and I was a supporter of President Ford. The media had fun with the overnight stay, trying to sort out how the Ford operatives would react to my invitation to the Reagans to spend a night in the hills of east Tennessee.

I competed against him in 1980 for the right to carry the Republican banner in the presidential election. He won, and I did not. Within a few months, I found myself standing with him as the majority leader in the U.S. Senate, committing to carry the agenda that he laid out for the country.

I had a notion that another person should be sitting in the Oval Office—me. In announcing my bid for the presidency in 1979, I said that for America to regain its greatness, the country needs "a president who can unite the people, chart a new course, and launch a new generation of confidence." It turned out that these words and phrases reflected the character and the essence of Ronald Reagan.

From his first days in office in 1981, I found that Ronald Reagan had a central core of convictions that focused his attention, his direction, and his leadership. Washington may expect a president to be mired down in details, but for President Reagan, that was not why he ran for the country's highest office or what he expected to achieve as its chief executive. He was comfortable with who he was and what he wanted to accomplish.

With a new Republican majority in the United States Senate, President Reagan laid out an agenda to move the country ahead. An early vote on budget reconciliation that led to the Reagan economic revolution stands out as the defining test for his new Republican majority and his direction for America. What I may have at one point termed "a riverboat gamble" turned out to be the right course. The cornerstone of Reagan's economic policy was curbing government spending coupled with tax reductions.

When he was elected president, the country was saddled with double-digit interest rates, high inflation, and unemployment. In dozens of White House meetings and sessions held in the Capitol with bipartisan congressional leaders, President Reagan laid out his approach and listened to differing points of view with an open mind. In crafting legislative solutions, President Reagan realized that if 80 percent could be achieved on the first pass, take it. The other 20 percent could be picked up later.

The most remarkable thing about him was his constant ability to surprise. This is how, as a consummate Washington insider, I remember Ronald Reagan. His first term as president put the nation's economy back on track and restored the respect for America across the world. As the leader in the U.S. Senate for his first term in office, I found him to be a reliable partner.

He stood tall for the things that he believed in and did not hesitate in the face of opposition to remain steadfast to his core convictions. He reached outside of Washington and touched the core of America to build his coalition for change.

In 1987, our paths crossed once more.

I recall vividly his request that I return to service, but as his chief of staff—not exactly how I imagined serving in the White House. But the president asked, and I accepted. I have never known how you turn down the president of the United States.

From the first days as his chief of staff, there was no doubt that Ronald Reagan had things he wanted to accomplish. A crucial budget agreement was reached, and a significant arms-reduction treaty was signed that marked a redefining of the relationship between the United States and the Soviet Union.

Although he was no longer in office when the Berlin Wall—that iconic symbol of oppression—fell, his address to thousands of Germans at the Brandenburg Gate set in motion the tearing down of that concrete barrier, which scarred a country and separated families.

I got to know Ronald Reagan in a different way while serving as his chief of staff. He was a true patriot and considered it an honor to serve the American people. In his eyes, you could see the awe that a child from humble beginnings in the small town of Tampico, Illinois, could achieve the highest office in the country. He was a special man, with heartfelt compassion. He was an optimist who loved this country, its people, and the right for every man, woman, and child to be free.

For those who advocated the politics of no new ideas, no incentives to save and to work, and no firm security for the nation, he countered with, "Yes, we can have a brighter tomorrow." He said "yes" is the one word we understand because that "is what we have grown up with as a country."

Ronald Reagan had a special touch conveyed through his choice of words, which calmed a nation in times of trouble and disappointment and celebrated the greatness of things both large and small.

When he spoke to the nation and to the families of those lost in the shuttle *Challenger* tragedy in 1986, I recall his words describing those seven astronauts waving goodbye as they "slipped the surly bonds of earth . . . to touch the face of God."

Or as he stood on the windswept hill overlooking the steep cliff that American Rangers scaled some forty years earlier as part of the D-Day invasion. He called them the men "who took the cliffs. These are the champions who helped free a continent. These are the heroes who helped end a war."

He talked about the Shining City on the Hill, of a "divine plan that placed this great continent between two oceans to be sought out by those who have an abiding love of freedom and a special kind of courage."

And he loved to tell stories, sprinkling his speeches with one-liners. Humor helped him warm up a crowd and connect to his audience—the American people. As he told the Associated General Contractors of America in 1981, "Status quo, you know, is Latin for 'the mess we're in.'"

Over my career, I have had the privilege to know eight presidents of the United States—each have had their own particular strengths and weaknesses. Ronald Reagan understood what it took to be president—he knew where he wanted to go and how to get there.

In his later years, as his health took its toll, Ronald Reagan remained interested in the lives of his friends. I recall his good wishes and genuine happiness when I married "my Nancy" in 1996. As Alzheimer's disease entered his life, he did what one would have expected from the Great Communicator—he shared the news with his fellow citizens.

He was a great American. I am proud to have been his friend and to have had the opportunity to serve with him and for him.

—SENATOR HOWARD H. BAKER, JR.

Chapter One

THE LIFESAVER

Family Values

The first person to recognize that Ronald Reagan could be presidential timber was his father. Moments after his son was born, John Edward "Jack" Reagan looked at the baby and said, "He looks like a fat little Dutchman. But who knows, he might grow up to be president someday."

Those prescient words were spoken in the early morning hours on February 6, 1911, in a small apartment above a bank in Tampico, Illinois. There, after a difficult delivery, Nelle Wilson Reagan gave birth to a ten-pound boy. Originally, his parents planned to name him Donald, but when a cousin was given that name, Nelle and Jack decided to name their second son Ronald. It really did not matter much, because everyone called him Dutch.

The Reagans' first son, John Neil Reagan, who had been born almost two and a half years earlier, was not exactly thrilled by the arrival of a little brother. He had hoped for a sister. Like his brother, John would be known by a nickname, too. He was called Moon, because his haircut reminded people of

Ronald Reagan, born February 6, 1911, in Tampico, Illinois.

the comic-strip character Moon Mullins. Doctors advised Nelle not to have any more children, which meant the Reagan family was complete.

Just over eight hundred people lived in Tampico when Dutch Reagan was born. There were a couple of stores, a church or two, and a railroad station. The Reagans' five-room apartment was on the town's main street. Although the house did not have running water or an indoor toilet, it was their home and the center of their lives.

Jack Reagan was of Irish ancestry and known as a great storyteller. His parents died before he was seven years old. An aunt raised him as an Irish Catholic, though as an adult he rarely attended church. He had a tendency to suspect the worst in people and did not trust established authority. He believed strongly in the rights of individuals and taught his boys that a person's skin color or religion did not matter— ambition and hard work determined a person's success. He was a natural salesman, especially good at selling shoes, and dreamed of one day having a store of his own.

Nelle Wilson tended to her home and boys, occasionally taking work as a seamstress. She was of Scots-English ancestry, and deeply religious. She rarely missed Sunday services at the Disciples of Christ Church. A natural optimist, Nelle taught Moon and Dutch the value of prayer and encouraged them to always look for the good in people. Whenever her schedule allowed it, she acted in local plays.

Jack and Nelle Reagan influenced Dutch in different but profound ways. On one point in particular, Jack and Nelle walked as one.

"My parents constantly drummed into me the importance of judging people as individuals. There was no more grievous sin at our household than a racial slur or other evidence of religious or racial intolerance," Ronald Reagan later recalled.

The Reagans moved a lot during Dutch's childhood. When he was just two, the family relocated to Chicago so Jack could take a job as a shoe salesman at Marshall Field's department store. They lived in the city, which was quite different from Tampico, with lots of people, sidewalks with gaslights, trolleys,

carriages, and even an automobile or two. Young Dutch enjoyed the bustle and excitement. But after less than two years, it was time to move again, this time to Galesburg, Illinois, where Jack took a job at another large department store. There, five-year-old Dutch taught himself to read. Before long, the family was on the road again, settling for a while in Monmouth, Illinois. They were there for Armistice Day, which was Dutch's first real exposure to soldiers and war.

Just after World War I ended, Jack, Nelle, Moon, and Dutch returned to Tampico, where Jack went back to work at the same shoe store he had left a few years earlier. His old boss promised to help him open his own shop. The shop was to be located in Dixon, Illinois, which meant yet another move for the Reagans. Ronald Reagan would later credit living in Dixon with helping make him the person he would become.

Ronald Reagan, one year old, with his brother, Neil, 1912.
Page 19 (left to right): Jack Reagan, early 1900s. Nelle Reagan with Ronald, 1915.

I learned from my father the value
of hard work and ambition,
and maybe a little something about
telling a story. From my mother,
I learned the value of prayer,
how to have dreams, and [the belief]
I could make them come true.

———

Ronald Reagan,
from An American Life

Natural-Born Performer

With a population of about ten thousand people, Dixon, Illinois, was quite different from the insular Tampico. The Reagan family arrived in 1920, when Dutch was nine years old. Dutch fell in love with the town immediately; it was his own version of heaven. Besides being much larger in scale than Tampico, it had a bustling main street lined with shops, churches, a post office, and several factories. Dairy farms dotted the town's periphery. A bucolic setting, it was where, as Reagan later recalled, he learned the standards and values that would guide him for the rest of his life.

In Dixon, the Reagan family could finally establish roots, make friends, and settle in. It was also in Dixon that Dutch learned some difficult life lessons. Chief among these was the fact that his father suffered from the disease of alcoholism. One incident in particular stuck in young Dutch's memory:

When I was eleven I came home from the YMCA one cold, blustery winter's night. My mother was gone on one of her sewing jobs and I expected the house to be empty. As I walked up the stairs, I nearly stumbled over a lump near the front door; it was Jack lying in the snow, his arms outstretched, flat on his back.

Ronald Reagan at age twelve, Dixon, Illinois, 1923.

I leaned over to see what was wrong and smelled whiskey. He had found his way home from a speakeasy and had just passed out right there. For a moment or two, I looked down at him and thought about continuing on into the house and going to bed, as if he weren't there. But I couldn't do it. When I tried to wake him he just snored—loud enough, I suspected, for the whole neighborhood to hear him. So I grabbed a piece of his overcoat, pulled it, and dragged him into the house, then put him to bed and never mentioned the incident to my mother.

Their father's drinking was a source of frustration and embarrassment for his sons, but Nelle urged them to be compassionate and understanding of their father's struggle. She explained to Dutch and Moon that their father had a sickness that he couldn't control, and she implored them to find the good in him when he wasn't drinking.

In Dixon, Dutch grew closer to his mother and came to share her religious beliefs, resulting in his baptism at the First Christian Church at the age of twelve. At his brother's urging, Moon was also baptized at the same time. When not working at home or the church, Nelle would act in community plays, as would Moon. They both encouraged Dutch to join them, but he was shy and reluctant. Eventually, he agreed to give the theater a try, and the applause he received for his debut on Dixon's small stage was unlike anything he had ever felt before. It changed him forever. His self-confidence soared, and he knew that acting would become an important part of his life.

Young Dutch's life took another positive turn when, quite by accident, he discovered he was nearsighted. He was playing with a pair of his mother's glasses, and when he put them on, the world came into sharp focus. All of a sudden, he could see the words on road signs, leaves on trees, and faces on people far away. Until that moment, he had just assumed everyone saw the world blurry. An eye doctor prescribed glasses, and Dutch was practically a new person, both in the classroom and on the athletic field.

Opposite, top: Ronald Reagan (second from left) and his teammates, Dixon, Illinois, 1927. **Opposite, bottom:** Formal portrait. Ronald is in the front row, left, 1919.

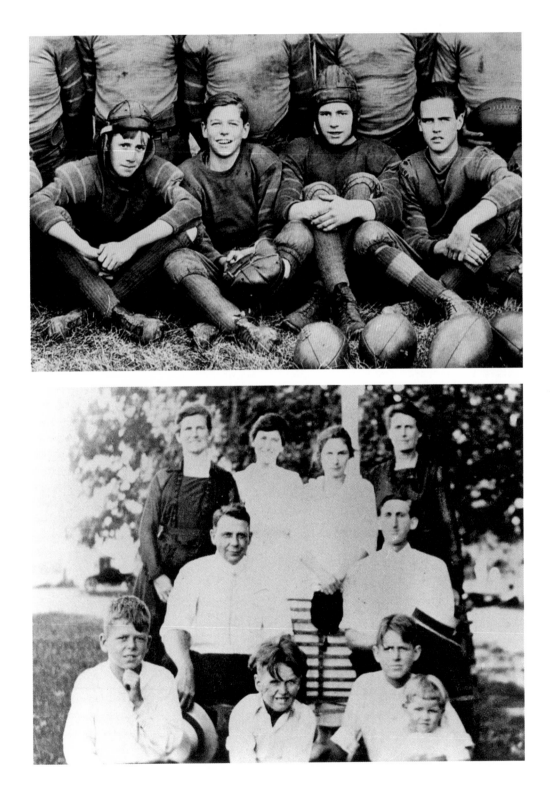

Football and swimming were two of Dutch's favorite sports when he entered Dixon High School in 1924. At a mere five foot three and 108 pounds, he was not big enough to make the football team in his freshman year. During the summer, he worked at a construction job laying floors, shingling roofs, and building homes. He was paid 35 cents an hour, and was able to build the muscles he needed to play football. It worked. Sort of. In his sophomore year, he made the team—in a new division for players who weighed less than 135 pounds—and was named captain. He continued to work hard, and by the time he was a junior he stood at 5 feet 10½ inches and weighed 160 pounds. He played right guard and tackle on the regular varsity team for his last two years of high school. He was also captain of the school's swim team.

Not all of his extracurricular activities were on the field or in the pool. Theater was another important part of his life at Dixon High School. An English teacher, B. J. Frazer, encouraged him to perform for his class when reading essays, which eventually led Dutch to try out for student plays Frazer directed. By his senior year, Dutch was completely dedicated to acting. And in what turned out to be a harbinger of things

Portrait of the Y.M.C.A. band sponsored by the Kiwanis Club, Dixon, Illinois, 1923. Ronald Reagan is the drum major, front row, left.
Page 26: Ronald Reagan as a lifeguard on the Rock River, circa 1931.

to come, Dutch was elected president of the student body. He was busy, happy, and coming into his own.

In his second year of high school and continuing for seven summers, Dutch was employed as a lifeguard at Lowell Park, a swimming section of the Rock River. For fifteen dollars a day, which was later raised to twenty dollars, Dutch worked ten to twelve hours, seven days a week. Over the course of seven seasons, he saved seventy-seven lives. He kept track of each life saved by carving a notch into a log near the edge of the river, which he proudly showed off whenever he could. When the swimming section was empty, Dutch would ride the manager's horse. He found riding to be not only good exercise, but also a relaxing, almost therapeutic way to clear his mind and recharge his batteries. What started as occasional rides in Lowell Park eventually grew to become a lifelong love for horses and equestrianship.

Less than 7 percent of high school graduates went on to college when Dutch graduated from Dixon High School in 1928, but Dutch was determined to be in that percentage. While the Reagan family did not have the means to afford tuition, Dutch was undeterred. He took almost every job he could find and saved as much money as he could, but it still was not enough. Nonetheless, he wanted to continue his education and keep playing football, and he was determined to go to college. His heart was set on Eureka College, a Disciples of Christ school located just over 100 miles southeast of Dixon. His interest in Eureka was sparked by his admiration for a local star athlete who had gone there. And when Dutch's steady girlfriend from high school, Margaret Cleaver, told him she was going there, too, Dutch became more determined than ever. He would find a way to go to Eureka.

One of the proudest statistics
of my life is seventy-seven—
the number of people I saved during
those seven summers.

———

Ronald Reagan,
on being a lifeguard

Campus Leader

Dutch could hardly believe his eyes when he drove Margaret
to Eureka College for her freshman year. The campus was
even more impressive and majestic than he had imagined. He
knew it was where he belonged, and he didn't want to leave.
He decided to take advantage of being on campus to see what
might be possible, but knew he did not have enough money
for tuition, room, and board. He would need a scholarship to
make his dream come true. Without an appointment, but on a
mission, he went to see Eureka's president and football coach,
and he used what would later become his legendary powers
of persuasion to convince them to grant him a needy student
scholarship. They agreed, but pointed out that the scholarship
would apply only to tuition fees. He would need a job to cover
living expenses. That didn't matter to Dutch Reagan. He was
going to Eureka.

Margaret introduced him to one of the brothers at the Tau
Kappa Epsilon fraternity. He liked the group and was invited to
pledge and become a brother. He lived in the fraternity house,
where he earned money washing dishes and serving tables.

Formal yearbook portrait, 1932.

He was so fond of the school that he persuaded his brother, Neil, to follow him there in 1929.

Dutch felt comfortable at Eureka College. He liked the fact that it was small and provided an opportunity for everyone to be part of things and to get to know each other. The school's intimate environment gave Dutch the opportunity to befriend fellow students and participate in a variety of extracurricular activities that he otherwise may have been remiss to try at a larger university. "I think I would have fallen back in the crowd and never discovered things about myself that I did at Eureka," he later surmised. Not that it was possible for Dutch Reagan to fall back in the crowd. Handsome, confident, and blessed with athleticism, he was a natural-born leader.

In his freshman year, he got his first taste of leadership when he ended up in charge of a student protest against a proposal by Eureka's president to cut faculty and some programs. While he never intended to head up the strike, he became the de facto leader after a rousing speech he made at a student rally. Students refused to attend classes, but their professors marked them as being present. After a week of rabble-rousing and mass confusion among staff and students alike, Eureka's president resigned and things returned to normal.

When he was not taking on the administration, Dutch enjoyed a wide range of extracurricular activities, with athletics being especially important. Just like at Dixon High School, football was first and foremost. He was a guard and earned varsity letters three of his four years. He also lettered in swimming and track.

Ronald Reagan, Eureka College football team, circa 1929.

It was at Eureka College that Dutch's dream of being a movie actor was born. He credits Ellen Marie Johnson, an English professor who served as faculty advisor to the theater arts after-school program, with encouraging him to try out for roles in school productions. As a result, he appeared in more than a dozen plays. More important, Johnson arranged for Eureka to participate in a prestigious college play competition at Northwestern University. After an outstanding performance there, the head of Northwestern's speech department told Dutch he should think about making acting his career. Dutch was thrilled because ever since his days in Dixon, when he would spend hours in the local movie theater, he had been in love with the cinema.

In addition to acting, he was president of the Boosters Club and a cheerleader for the basketball team. He stayed active in campus politics, serving two years in the student senate, and was elected student body president in his senior year.

All of that was, of course, in addition to his academic studies. He would joke later about having majored in "extracurricular activities," but Dutch Reagan officially majored in economics and social science at Eureka College, graduating with a bachelor of arts degree in 1932.

Opposite: Eureka College football team, 1928. Ronald Reagan is sitting, fourth from the right.

People ask me if in looking back
at my college years I can remember
any inkling that I would one day run
for president. Well, actually,
the thought first struck me
on graduation day when the president
handed me my diploma and asked,
"Are you better off today than you were
four years ago?"

———

Ronald Reagan,
remarks at Eureka College, Eureka, Illinois,
February 6, 1984

Aspiring Actor

The country was in the beginning years of the Great Depression when Dutch Reagan graduated from college. There were very few jobs, especially for people with no work experience.

He knew what he wanted to do. He wanted to be an actor, and the first step to accomplishing that, in Dutch's mind, was to find a job as a sports announcer on the radio. After a final season as a lifeguard at Lowell Park, Dutch drove with his brother to Eureka College, and from there hitchhiked to Chicago in search of a radio station that would give him a job.

He knocked on door after door, but no one would hire him. Most station directors would not even talk to him. One person who did, however, was the program director of the local NBC station, who told him that looking in Chicago for a first job was a bad idea, because stations there could afford to hire experienced announcers. She suggested he look in smaller markets, where lack of experience would not matter as much. Then, after spending some time honing his skills, he could come back to Chicago and try again. The plan made sense, but it left Dutch discouraged. Almost out of money, he hitchhiked back to Dixon to look for whatever job he could get. He interviewed for

Ronald Reagan on horseback, circa 1930s.

a position managing the sporting goods department at the local Montgomery Ward, and he left the store thinking that the job, which paid $12.50 a week, would be his. After all, he had excelled at sports and promised the store manager that he would be the best sporting goods department manager he had ever seen. A few days later, Dutch was told that someone else—a former high school basketball star—had been hired. Dutch felt defeated, and turned to his father for advice. What Jack lacked in job stability, he compensated with fatherly wisdom and a dreamer's sense of passion. His son told him of his goal to be a sports announcer, and what the NBC program director had recommended. Jack listened patiently and was sympathetic to Dutch's plight. He understood what it meant to have a vision, and he wanted to help. So he offered to let his son use the family car to go to some nearby small towns to see if he could get his first break.

After striking out with several small stations in Illinois, Dutch crossed the Mississippi River into Iowa, where his first stop was in Davenport, at station WOC. The station had been founded by the owner of the Palmer School of Chiropractic, Colonel B. J. Palmer, and the call letters stood for World of Chiropractic. Dutch met with the station's program director, only to find out that the job for an announcer had just been filled. The program director acted as though it was Dutch's fault that he had not applied sooner. Disappointed and even a little angry, Dutch walked away from the meeting, purposely grumbling loudly about how hard it was to get a job as a sports announcer if no one would hire him at a radio station. The program director's ears perked up, and he chased after Dutch, telling him he had not realized the young man was interested in sports.

When asked if he knew anything about football, Dutch recounted his high school and college experience with such accuracy and exuberance that he was immediately taken to an unoccupied studio for a test. He gave a stirring account of a game he had played at Eureka, vividly describing the scene, calling the plays, and even offering commentary on the players. He was hired on the spot to broadcast the Iowa-Minnesota homecoming game a few days later, for which he received five dollars and bus fare. After his first broadcast, the program director hired him to broadcast the three remaining games on Iowa's schedule, doubling his pay to ten dollars. Dutch Reagan was officially employed as a sports announcer. Unfortunately, his happiness would be short-lived.

At the end of the season, WOC had no spots to fill, so Dutch headed back to Dixon to look for a job—again. Spirits down, he expected he would have to wait until the summer for work, when he would lifeguard again at Lowell Park.

When he got home, Jack made a point of telling his son that there were things happening in the country far more important than college football games. Jack was an outspoken Democrat —one of a very few in Dixon—and he was excited about the election of Franklin D. Roosevelt. He expected Roosevelt to help working people and get the country back on track.

Like his father, Dutch was a strong supporter of FDR. In 1932, he proudly cast his first vote for him and the entire Democratic ticket. Dutch was impressed by Roosevelt's quick and decisive actions to deal with the economic crisis facing the country and was drawn to Roosevelt's skills as a communicator.

Miraculously, in February, WOC asked him to come back to Davenport to fill a vacant announcer position at a salary of one hundred dollars per month. He left the next day. Things did not go very well. He really did not have much experience as a radio announcer, and it showed. He got help and improved quickly, but it wasn't long before he was in trouble again. This time, it was not for how he said things—it was for how he didn't.

Dutch's career at WOC was almost cut short when he failed to plug a local mortuary after playing the romantic song "I Love You Truly." He thought that to do so would be in poor taste. In exchange for an on-air mention, the mortuary had provided organ music for one of the radio station's programs, an arrangement of which Dutch was not aware. Naturally, the mortuary's director complained to the station manager, who, recalling Dutch's earlier on-air difficulties, fired him. Dutch was asked to stay on for a few days to help train his replacement, which he agreed to do. In a twist of irony, when his replacement heard what had happened to Dutch, he demanded a contract to provide job security. The station refused and gave Dutch his

old job back. It was supposed to be just until a new replacement could be found, but after more coaching, Dutch improved to the point where the station no longer sought to replace him.

Not long after that, Dutch was asked to broadcast one of the country's top track relays on WHO, WOC's sister station in Des Moines. The former track star did so well that he was offered a position as sports announcer for WHO, which had become one of NBC's most powerful stations—exactly where Dutch wanted to be.

Dutch spent four years at station WHO in Des Moines, covering all types of sporting events. He later counted this time as the most pleasant in his life. After all, at the tender age of twenty-two, he had already accomplished his dream of becoming a sports announcer. He was earning good money—seventy-five dollars a week—and had achieved the kind of fame that not only boosted his ego but also brought paid invitations to speaking engagements. With the extra income, Dutch was able to send money to his parents—no small feat during the Great Depression.

Among the many sports events Dutch announced while at WHO were Chicago Cubs baseball games, even though he was nowhere near the stadium. Instead, sitting in the studio in Des Moines, he relied on Morse code messages from a telegraph

Ronald Reagan, sportscaster for station WHO, 1930.

operator in the stadium press box, who reported on each pitch and play. The messages came over a wire, were decoded and typed out by another telegraph operator in the Des Moines studio, and handed to Dutch for broadcast as if he were live on the scene. He would "describe" the weather, the looks on the players' faces, fan reactions, and anything else he could think of to make his listeners feel as if they were there. For the most part, the system worked well. Once, however, the wire went dead and Dutch was forced to improvise for more than seven minutes while waiting for the connection to be reestablished.

During the winter, the Cubs trained at Catalina Island, located just twenty-six miles off the coast of southern California. Like the team, the island was owned by the Wrigley chewing gum family. Neither its sunny weather, especially when compared to winters in Iowa, nor its proximity to Hollywood were lost on Dutch, who still wanted to be a movie actor. So he came up with a scheme to get himself to Catalina for free. He proposed to his bosses at WHO that he could use his vacation time to "cover" the team in Catalina, as long as the station paid his travel expenses. To his delight, WHO agreed. Somehow he neglected to mention that he would earn a little extra money writing articles for small newspapers there, too.

It was on his third annual trip to Catalina that Dutch was able to do what he had been dreaming of doing for years: go to Hollywood to see if he could make it big in the movies. In Los Angeles, he looked up Joy Hodges, a friend with whom he had worked at WHO. Joy was singing with a band at night while also trying to get on the silver screen. She said she knew an agent who would be able to give her old friend a realistic assessment of whether or not he had a chance at a career in movies. She set up a meeting for the next day.

When Dutch Reagan went to see the agent, Bill Meiklejohn, he was uncharacteristically nervous. Here he was about to find out if his lifelong ambition was real or nothing more than a pipe dream, and to make matters worse, he was having trouble seeing because Joy had been adamant that he not wear glasses to the meeting. Dutch made his pitch. Meiklejohn said nothing. When Dutch asked him if he thought he had a shot, Meiklejohn just looked at him. Dutch thought he would be politely thanked and shown the door. Instead, Meiklejohn picked up his phone and called Max Arnow, a casting director at Warner Bros. Meiklejohn described Reagan as "another Robert Taylor." Arnow said there was only one Robert Taylor, but he was willing to see Dutch anyhow. When they met, the casting director was taken by Dutch's good looks, charm, and especially his smooth voice. A screen test was scheduled.

Dutch returned to Catalina, where he spent every spare moment studying the script he had been given. A few days later, he took a boat back to Los Angeles for the screen test. This was it: Whatever happened next could determine his entire future. When Arnow saw the screen test, he knew that he had found a star. He called Meiklejohn and told him he planned to show it to studio boss Jack Warner.

Dutch could hardly believe what was happening. It was exactly what he had hoped and worked for as far back as he could remember. Before he could get the results of his screen test, Dutch had to return to Iowa to resume broadcasting Cubs' baseball games. He did not want to leave Los Angeles, but had no choice.

He would not be gone for long. Less than forty-eight hours after arriving back in Des Moines, he received a telegram from Meiklejohn telling him that Warner Bros. had offered a seven-year contract for two hundred dollars a week. He rushed to the Western Union office, where he sent a telegram back saying, "Sign before they change their minds."

A few weeks later, Dutch was in a Nash convertible headed west.

"That trip across the country, with the top of my car open to the wind and the sun shining on my head, was one of the highest of the highs. I was on my way to Hollywood," Reagan would later say fondly.

Warner Bros. planned to cast him in a picture right away, but not before making a few changes. First, his hair. It was short and parted down the middle. It would not do. A studio stylist said it looked like a bowl-cut. Next, his wardrobe. Because he

Ronald Reagan, on the Warner Bros. studio lot, early 1940s.

had a relatively small head, big shoulders, and a short neck, he would have to wear custom-designed shirts. Dutch did not feel too badly about that when he found out Jimmy Cagney had the same "problem," and was pleased that the studio would use Cagney's shirtmaker for him.

The biggest change the studio wanted to make was to his name. For reasons he never fully understood, studio publicists decided that Dutch could not be the name of a movie star. Without offering any rationale and in a tone of absolute certainty, one flatly stated, "You can't put 'Dutch Reagan' on a marquee." At a meeting to discuss the issue, Dutch suggested using his given name of Ronald, pointing out that it was well-known to many radio listeners in the Midwest. The publicists looked at him and started saying it over and over to each other. Ronald Reagan. Ronald Reagan. Ronald Reagan. After a few minutes, one said he liked it and the matter was settled. Ronald Reagan would henceforth be known as Ronald Reagan.

When Ronald Reagan drove onto the Warner Bros. lot in Burbank for the first time in June 1937, he was almost overwhelmed by feelings of excitement and anxiety. He was about to embark on the career he had been fantasizing about since childhood, yet he kept having to ask himself what he was doing there. After all, it had been several years since he had acted in anything, and that was only a few plays in college. He was worried because a clause in his contract allowed the studio to fire him after six months if they did not like his work, despite the public announcement of a "long-term" contract. Would he make the grade, or would he end up disappointing the studio and be sent packing? Was this skinny twenty-six-year-old kid from Iowa really worthy of being in the company of such legends as Errol Flynn, Olivia de Havilland, and Pat O'Brien?

Seeing his own screen test on that first day did little to calm his fears.

But a funny thing happened on the way to Hollywood: Ronald Reagan became a movie star.

Opposite, top: Ronald Reagan with his parents, California, circa 1937. **Opposite, bottom:** Casual snapshot of Ronald Reagan, poised and confident, 1941. **Page 44:** Ronald Reagan visiting East High School in Des Moines, Iowa, circa 1936.

Chapter Two

THE LEADING MAN

Film Star

Hollywood operated on what was known as the "studio system" when Ronald Reagan began his career in "the picture business," as he called it. Eight mega-studios—Fox, Loew's (which owned Metro-Goldwyn-Mayer), Paramount, RKO, Universal, Columbia, United Artists, and of course, Warner Bros., made movies on their own lots and distributed them through theaters they owned. Ronald Reagan likened the system to "an old-fashioned candy store, where they make it in the back and sell it in the front." Although the U.S. Supreme Court would eventually rule against the studio system, when Reagan was in Hollywood that's largely how things worked.

During the 1940s and 1950s, there were basically two kinds of films: "A" movies, which had big budgets and big-name stars, and "B" movies, with smaller budgets and lesser-known actors. "B" movie actors were usually under long-term contracts to a particular studio, and their films were essentially tests studios used to gauge whether or not an actor could effectively build a profitable fan base and fill theaters.

An early publicity shot of Ronald Reagan, circa 1950.

Ronald Reagan was on the "B" team, which was fine with him—for a while. His first film was *Love Is on the Air*, in which he played a radio announcer. In preparation for the role, Reagan spent the day before filming going over the script with a dialogue coach. While playing a radio announcer might have seemed like typecasting, Warner Bros.' newest player was anything but calm during his debut.

Though he had appeared on stage several times before, his theatrical experiences had been limited to the college circuit, a far cry from the professionalism and talent expected from one of Hollywood's biggest studios. Fighting the urge to skip town, Reagan later recalled, "Nothing I'd ever experienced . . . nothing I'd ever been through, had ever produced in me the kind of jitters I felt when I stepped onto Stage Eight at Warner Bros. that morning."

But a veteran character actor told him not to worry, and his anxiety disappeared the moment the director shouted, "Action!" Ronald Reagan delivered his lines exactly as the script called for—on the first take. The rest of the filming went smoothly, and Reagan began to think he might make it in the movies after all.

It would be four months before *Love Is on the Air* was released and Reagan would receive his first reviews. During that time he made his second picture, *Sergeant Murphy*, based on a true story about a horse that won Britain's Grand National steeplechase race. Again, it was a role that seemed custom-made for him: He played a cavalryman. As focused as he was on giving a great performance, he could not get his mind off the reviews that would soon be in for his first movie. He need not have worried.

Reviews for his performance in *Love Is on the Air* were great. The all-important *Hollywood Reporter* said, "*Love Is on the Air* presents a new leading man, Ronald Reagan, who is a natural, giving one of the best first-picture performances Hollywood has offered in many a day." Warner Bros. renewed his contract for another six months and gave him a raise. Sweetest of all was the fact that he could now afford to bring his parents to California.

Ronald Reagan made thirty-one movies for Warner Bros. in the first year and a half of his contract. They were all "B"

pictures, but he was proud of most of them, and the studio was happy with his work. He was developing a fan base and enjoying life in sunny Southern California. He was also ready to start a family.

In 1940, perhaps falling victim to what some called "leading lady-itis"—a condition in which male actors fall in love with their female costars—Ronald Reagan married Jane Wyman, another Warner Bros. contract player, with whom he had appeared in William Keighley's 1938 film *Brother Rat*. Though their marriage brought two wonderful children, daughter Maureen, and son Michael, they eventually divorced in 1948.

Ronald Reagan, in a movie still from *Love Is on the Air*, 1936.

While he was quite pleased with how his career was developing, Ronald Reagan wanted to make the move from the "B" list to the "A" list, and he had an idea about how to do it. For many years, Reagan had been interested in the life story of Knute Rockne, the Notre Dame football coach who revolutionized the game of football and later died in a plane crash. Reagan thought this story was the perfect vehicle for a movie. Pat O'Brien would be perfect in the role of Rockne, and Reagan would play George Gipp, better known as the Gipper, the legendary Notre Dame player, who died two weeks after his final game. He shared his idea with almost anyone who would listen and even began working on a screenplay.

No one was more surprised than Reagan the day he picked up *Variety*—Hollywood's top trade paper—and read that Warner Bros. was planning a movie based on the life story of Knute Rockne, starring none other than Pat O'Brien. To make matters worse, Reagan learned that the studio had already screen-tested actors for the role of George Gipp. He was beside himself. He sought out the movie's producer and told him he wanted to be considered for the role. The producer looked him up and down, and said he was sorry, but Reagan just did not look the part of a legendary college football player. He was too small. Reagan protested, pointing out that he actually weighed more than Gipp did when he played for Notre Dame, but the producer was unmoved.

Reagan would not give up. Remembering something a cameraman once told him—producers and directors need to see things to believe them—Reagan sped home and rummaged around to find a picture of himself in his college football uniform. He then raced back to the producer's office at the studio and showed him the photo. Other than asking if he could hang on to it for a while, the producer gave Reagan no hint of a reaction. The hopeful would-be Gipper left the studio not knowing what to think.

Reagan headed home and, after barely an hour, he received a call asking him to report to the studio early the next morning to test for the part of George Gipp. To Reagan's delight, the next day the producer called to say the part was his—and Pat O'Brien would play Rockne.

Of all the roles Ronald Reagan played in the dozens of movies he made, there is none with which he is more closely identified, or for which he is better remembered, than that of George Gipp in *Knute Rockne All American*. The scene of Gipp on his deathbed, talking to Rockne and encouraging his teammates—"to win one for the Gipper"—has become an important part of Reagan's legacy.

Not only did the movie confer on him the nickname of the Gipper, it moved Reagan from the "B" list to the "A" list, just as he had hoped. In his first A-list film, *Santa Fe Trail*, he costarred with none other than Errol Flynn.

As his career blossomed, Reagan took great pleasure in being able to buy a house for his parents, who had never owned a home—no one in his family had. He was especially happy to be able to get his father a job at the studio handling his fan mail. Jack's poor health had left him unable to work for a long time, and he welcomed the opportunity to get back to doing something productive. Unfortunately, he was not able to do so for long. In May 1941, he died of a heart attack at the age of fifty-eight.

Ironically, 1941 also brought one of the high points of Ronald Reagan's Hollywood career. His performance as Drake McHugh in the critically-acclaimed *Kings Row* was widely viewed as his best ever and had industry insiders talking about an Academy Award. But as luck would have it, that same year Warner Bros. made *Yankee Doodle Dandy*, which starred Jimmy Cagney as George M. Cohan, and the studio decided to put all of its efforts behind that picture.

Kings Row's defining scene occurs when McHugh, played by Reagan, awakes to find that both of his legs have been amputated by a sadistic surgeon who wants to punish him for dating his daughter. Reagan screams, "Where's the rest of me?" to his wife, played by costar Ann Sheridan.

The look of horror on Reagan's face and the sheer terror in his voice are nothing short of chilling. Per his usual style, he had done the scene in one take. So immortal were those lines that he chose them for the title of his first autobiography, *Where's the Rest of Me?*

Page 55: Ronald Reagan punting midair in a movie still from the 1940 film, *Knute Rockne All American*.

Sometime when the team is up
against it and the breaks are beating
the boys, tell them to go out there
with all they've got and win
just one for the Gipper!

Ronald Reagan
as George "The Gipper" Gipp in
Knute Rockne All American

Even the usually modest Reagan was a fan of his performance in *Kings Row*, and he later credited it with taking his career to a new level, saying, "*Kings Row* is the finest picture I ever appeared in, and it elevated me to the degree of stardom I had dreamed of when I had arrived in Hollywood four years earlier."

Years later, Reagan would recall that his other costar in *Kings Row*, Bob Cummings, displayed what could have been psychic powers when he told people on the set that someday he would vote for Reagan for president.

Not long after the release of *Kings Row*, the Japanese attacked Pearl Harbor, and Reagan's rising status as an "A"-list star was placed on hold when he was ordered to report for active duty in the U.S. Army at the San Francisco Port of Embarkation at Fort Mason. Because of his nearsightedness, he was not able to serve in active combat. He spent the majority of his time in the army assigned to the Eighteenth Army Air Force Unit, otherwise known as the First Motion Picture Unit, where he was involved with the production of military training films.

Toward the end of the war, his unit received classified films that had been shot by U.S. troops in Europe and showed the brutality of the Nazi concentration camps. Reagan was horrified by the ghastly images. Remembering that after World War I, there had been talk that some in America may have fallen victim to false propaganda about the Central Powers, Captain Reagan made and kept a copy of one of the films. He was determined that if he had anything to say about it, no one would later be able to deny what had happened in Germany, because he had proof.

Such an occasion arose several years later when a producer and his wife came to his home for dinner, and the conversation turned to the war. They wondered aloud whether what had been said about the Holocaust was really true. Reagan excused himself from the table, retrieved his 16-millimeter projector, rolled down a screen, and showed the film.

The scene that unfurled on the screen was simply heartbreaking and emotionally wrenching. A group of Jews

Ronald Reagan and costars, in a movie still from *Kings Row*, 1942.

were attempting to escape the concentration camp, only to be mowed down by German machine guns. It was a brutal display of violence, and was made all the more dramatic by the raw quality of the film footage. No one in the room had ever experienced or seen anything quite so intense.

When the lights came back on, the producer and his wife were in tears.

Another lesson—albeit a lighter one—from his days in the army that would make a lasting impression on Reagan was how downright inefficient government bureaucracy could be, especially trying when it came to personnel matters. It was not his first exposure to government waste; he had seen some of that when his father worked for the federal government years earlier in Dixon. What especially frustrated him while in the army was how difficult it was to remove incompetent or unneeded workers. Since bureaucrats were paid on the basis of how many people they managed, they were reluctant to let anyone go. In fact, their inclination was to increase the size of their operations. Years later, Reagan would often say that "the first rule of the bureaucracy is protect the bureaucracy."

Captain Ronald Reagan was honorably discharged from the U.S. Army in 1945. He happily went back to Hollywood to continue making movies. He had a contract with Warner Bros., but also worked for Paramount, MGM, RKO, and Universal as a free agent. He also returned to a leadership position with the Screen Actors Guild. Reagan was first elected to its board in 1941 before the war and became a vice president in 1946. When a change in the bylaws caused several SAG board members to resign in 1947, Ronald Reagan was elected as its president. He would go on to serve as the SAG's head from 1947 to 1952, and again in 1959. Protracted labor-management disputes, contract disagreements, and a strike all demanded his attention during that period. He proved himself a tough negotiator on behalf of his union and a very effective leader.

Ronald Reagan in military uniform, Fort MacArthur, California, circa 1941.

Captain Ronald Reagan at work, circa 1943.

Ronald Reagan, back row, second from left, with team members from the
Motion Picture Unit Basketball Team, Fort Roach, circa 1943.

Leading man Ronald Reagan posing for fans with his mother, 1949. **Opposite, top:** Lt. Ronald Reagan on the set of a U.S. Army Air Force documentary, circa 1942. **Opposite, middle:** Ronald Reagan with his brother, Neil, 1943. **Opposite, bottom:** Ronald Reagan with his first wife, Jane Wyman, and children, Michael and Maureen, mid 1940s.

Hollywood Insider
and Family Man

One of the most delicate issues facing Hollywood during the late 1940s was the fear of Communist infiltration in the motion picture industry. Like his father, Ronald Reagan believed deeply in freedom and the rights of individuals, so was a fierce anti-Communist. He viewed the Communist threat as real and testified before the House Committee on Un-American Activities in Washington in 1947. At the same time, he was genuinely concerned that the motion picture business was being swept up in a hysteria that viewed it as being sympathetic to Communists. He wanted to make certain that reputations were not ruined by rumor or innuendo. He believed that one of his most important responsibilities as president of the SAG was to protect its members from unwarranted accusations.

One member with reason to be concerned was an actress named Nancy Davis, who was under contract to MGM. Her name had turned up on the rosters of several groups believed to be Communist fronts, and she was receiving invitations to meetings she knew nothing about and of which she wanted no part. Distraught, she went to director Mervyn LeRoy, who offered to call his friend, the president of the SAG, to see if things could be straightened out. It didn't take long for Ronald Reagan to figure out that there was more than one Nancy Davis in Hollywood; it was this "other" Nancy Davis who

was believed to be involved with the pro-Communist groups. Reagan told LeRoy that MGM's Nancy Davis's name was clear, and she had nothing to worry about. Reagan had no way of knowing it at the time, but Nancy Davis was not one to easily stop worrying.

Reagan's assurance to LeRoy was not good enough for her. She was still concerned that some people might wrongly think she had Communist leanings. LeRoy called Reagan again and suggested he take her to dinner to offer reassurance that everything was all right. He told Reagan that Nancy Davis would not rest until she heard it directly from the president of the SAG, and said the two might even enjoy getting to know each other. Reagan was agreeable to having dinner with a pretty young actress and called to set it up.

Ronald Reagan and Nancy Davis dining, circa 1951. **Page 66:** Nancy Davis and Ronald Reagan in formal wear, early 1950s.

It was because of the [Screen Actors]
Guild and, more precisely, because I was
president that I found myself standing
before an apartment door in Westwood
one pleasant fall evening. When that
door opened, I found all the rest of
me I needed to find to give me more
happiness than any one person could
possibly deserve.

———

Ronald Reagan,
on meeting Nancy Davis

They went to a nice restaurant on the Sunset Strip and talked about her problem. Just as LeRoy had said, Davis was very upset about the whole situation. Ironically, Reagan suggested she might want to change her name, but she protested. She was and would remain Nancy Davis. As one who had almost had his name changed for far less serious reasons, the former Dutch Reagan fully understood. Eventually, they moved on to other topics. She told him about her father, a prominent neurosurgeon in Chicago, and her mother, a Broadway actress. He told her about life in Dixon. While they had both claimed to have early calls the following morning, after dinner they went to a nearby club to see singer Sophie Tucker perform—twice—and ended up staying out until three in the morning. Neither mentioned early calls again.

The following night, they went to dinner again, this time in Malibu. While they had a good time and enjoyed each other's company, they continued to date other people. They saw one another occasionally. This arrangement lasted for some time until Reagan, not wanting to be alone while giving a speech in San Diego, asked Nancy to accompany him. The trip cemented their relationship. Soon after, they were a couple, but kept their relationship secret from all but a few close friends and family. His proposal over dinner at their favorite restaurant, Chasen's, was right to the point: "Let's get married." Her reply was even more succinct: "Let's."

Since they were both celebrities, they chose to keep their engagement and wedding plans secret. On March 4, 1952, they were married in a small, private ceremony at The Little Brown Church in the Valley, with Bill Holden serving as best man and his wife, Ardis, as the matron of honor. The next day the newlyweds drove to Phoenix, where they joined Nancy's parents, Loyal and Edith Davis, to celebrate. As a devoted son-in-law, Reagan sent Nancy's mother flowers every Mother's Day to thank her for her daughter, who had made him so happy.

Soon after she was married, Nancy Davis—now Nancy Reagan—asked to be released from her contract at MGM so she

The newlyweds cutting their wedding cake, 1952.

could turn her attention to her new life. Toward the end of the year, the Reagans welcomed their first child together, daughter Patricia Ann.

While his personal life could not have been better, Ronald Reagan's movie career was not going as well as he had hoped it would. Some of his films were good, but there were others he was sorry he had made. Though initially reluctant because he thought it would destroy his box office appeal, to help with finances, Reagan began appearing on television programs, one of which indirectly led to a career change no one could have predicted.

In 1954, he was hired to host the *General Electric Theater* program, a dramatic anthology featuring a different story and cast every week. Ronald Reagan was a perfect fit, and his timing could not have been better. He became part of the golden age of television. Being seen every Sunday evening quickly made him a familiar and popular national figure.

Part of the job included traveling to GE plants around the country and speaking to employees, usually about Hollywood. In addition, he would often address local civic organizations while in town. Over time, his speeches evolved from being just about Hollywood to exposing the dangers of a big government. Audience response was phenomenal.

He was also still making movies. For one, the former Nancy Davis came out of "retirement" to appear as his costar in *Hellcats of the Navy*, a World War II story in which Reagan played submarine captain Casey Abbott, and Davis played a nurse for whom he had romantic feelings. It was the only time they appeared in a picture together.

Their second child, Ronald Prescott, was born in 1958, and although Reagan's movie star days were beginning to draw to a close, life was good for the Reagan family. As Reagan later explained:

In Hollywood I'd found more than I'd ever expected life to give me. For many, many reasons, these were very happy years for Nancy and me. My income from General Electric had enabled us to build a dream house overlooking the Pacific Ocean, which GE stuffed with

Movie poster for *Hellcats of the Navy,* 1957.

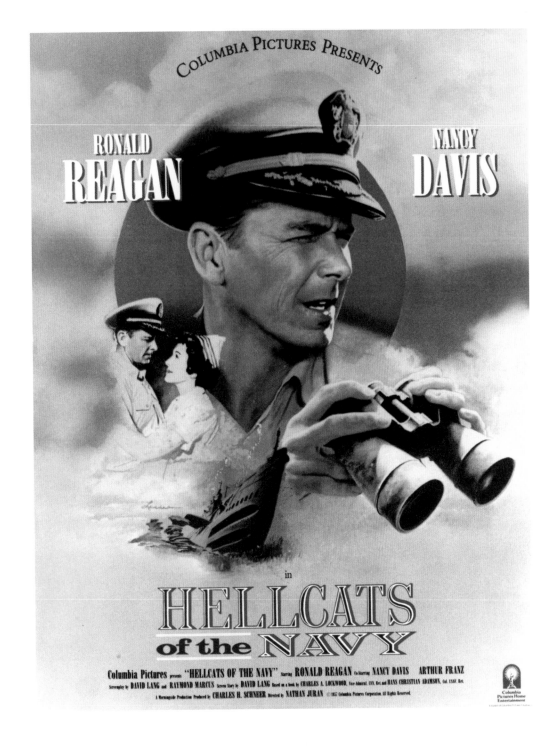

every imaginable electric gadget. We also bought a 350-acre ranch in the Santa Monica mountains north of Los Angeles, which we loved. And, although GE kept me on the road a lot, there were long stretches of my life during that period when my daily routine focused entirely on my family, our ranch, and a horse.

Ronald Reagan remained politically active during this period, but he was becoming increasingly uncomfortable with the positions of the Democratic Party, to which he had belonged his entire life. He found that he was making speeches about what government should and should not do, but then, out of party loyalty, voted for the people doing the very things he said were wrong.

Being a Democrat, he campaigned for both Harry Truman and Hubert Humphrey in 1948. In 1950, he supported Democrat Helen Gahagan Douglas, Richard Nixon's opponent in the U.S. Senate race in California. In 1952, Reagan sent a telegram to Dwight D. Eisenhower urging him to seek the presidency as a Democrat, but Eisenhower opted for the Republican Party. That didn't matter to Reagan, who still thought he was the best person for the job. For the first time in his life, Reagan voted for a Republican.

By 1960, Ronald Reagan's positions had progressed to the point where he supported Nixon's candidacy for the presidency. Feeling much more in tune with positions taken by the Republican Party, Reagan intended to switch his registration, but at Nixon's request, held off so he could campaign as a Democrat for Nixon. Two years later, when again campaigning for Nixon, who this time was running for governor of California, Reagan crossed over and spoke at a Republican fund-raising event. Before Reagan finished his speech, a woman asked him if he had officially changed his party registration. He told her he would soon, but that response was not good enough for her. She said she was a registrar, and she walked to the podium to hand him a registration card. A few minutes later, Ronald Reagan was officially registered as a Republican.

In 1962, after a battle with what is now known as Alzheimer's disease, his mother, Nelle, died. Nelle had given her son strength and guidance throughout his life. Reagan threw himself into his work as he had never done before, renewed with the conviction that he could make a difference in the world.

In the early 1960s, Ronald Reagan gave speeches from one coast to the other. He was more popular than ever and received more invitations to speak than GE could handle. But there was a change in GE's top management, and the new team asked Reagan to go on the road to pitch the company's products instead. He believed that after having established a reputation as a speaker about important national issues, it wouldn't be right to "peddle toasters," but GE insisted, and when he said no, they canceled *General Electric Theater*.

Reagan was disappointed but knew he had made the right decision. Although he had almost entirely made the transition from a movie star to a leading political voice, he still felt a tug toward the picture business. In 1964, Universal asked him to make what would be his last film. It was a remake of *The Killers*, which had originally starred Burt Lancaster in 1946. Reagan had never played a "bad guy" before and was reluctant at first, but the studio eventually persuaded him. Perhaps because moviegoers did not like seeing Reagan as a villain, the movie did not set any box office records.

All in all, between 1937 and 1964, Ronald Reagan appeared in fifty-three Hollywood movies. His costars ranged from Hollywood greats to a precocious chimpanzee in *Bedtime for Bonzo*. He was proud of his time in Hollywood, and he bristled when derided as being "just an actor" and therefore somehow unqualified to do anything else.

Soon after he finished making *The Killers*, Ronald Reagan was hired to host and occasionally act in the television series *Death Valley Days*. It was his kind of show. Filmed close to his house, he could often work in his regular ranch clothes. The job also left him time to make speeches and to campaign for Republican candidates. His personal life and his political life were happily intertwined.

The Reagan family at Ronald Prescott's christening, 1958.
Opposite, clockwise from top left: Ronald with his son, Ronald Prescott, Coronado, California, circa 1962; Ronald Reagan, Patti Davis, Nancy Reagan, and Ronald Prescott in front of the Christmas tree at the Reagan home in Pacific Palisades, California, 1960; Ronald Reagan posing casually with his daughter, Patti, in their backyard, circa 1958; Ronald Reagan reading a story to Ronald Prescott and Patti at Christmas, circa 1964.

Ronald Reagan on the set of the 1952 film *The Winning Team*.
Opposite: Ronald Reagan, swimming and diving at his home in
California, with Mrs. Reagan looking on, circa 1957.

Host of *General Electric Theater*, Ronald Reagan is posed with
portraits of stars who appeared on the show. **Opposite, top:**
Ronald Reagan at a plant, talking with GE employees, 1950s.
Opposite, bottom: Ronald Reagan as the character Frame Johnson
in the 1953 film *Law and Order*.

Ronald Reagan jumping his horse, with Nancy Reagan looking on, 1958.

The Reagans overlooking their Malibu Ranch property, 1958.

Rising Political Star

One politician who was anxious to have Ronald Reagan's
help was the Republican candidate for president in 1964,
Barry Goldwater, whom Reagan knew personally and liked.
Reagan was named cochairman of the Goldwater campaign in
California, and he traveled throughout the state raising funds
for the campaign and making speeches to rally the supporters.
One speech in particular would lead Ronald Reagan down a
path that would change history.

It was late summer when Reagan addressed a large
gathering of Republicans at the Coconut Grove nightclub in the
Ambassador Hotel in Los Angeles. As he had done hundreds
of times before, Reagan spoke of the perils of big, expanding
government, the inefficiency of bureaucracy, and the tendency
of the Democratic Party to favor expensive social programs.
He cited examples of how the government routinely wasted
taxpayers' money. He urged the audience to do everything
possible to help Barry Goldwater win the presidency. The
audience loved the speech . . . and Ronald Reagan.

Ronald Reagan giving a speech for the Goldwater campaign at the
International Hotel in Los Angeles, 1964.

As Reagan was leaving the room, a small group of people asked if he would join them for a few minutes at their table. Other than waiters and busboys clearing tables, they were the only people in the room. Someone asked Reagan if he would be willing to make the speech again on national television if they bought the airtime. Reagan did not know it at the time, but this group of supporters included some of the largest donors to the California Republican Party.

Reagan answered that if they really thought it would help the Goldwater campaign, he would be willing to do it, and he suggested it would be better delivered to a live audience of invited Republicans rather than recorded in an empty studio. They agreed. A few days later, they reported that they had enough money to buy airtime on NBC. Reagan taped the speech in a studio with an enthusiastic audience and left expecting it would be aired as planned.

A few days later, Barry Goldwater called to say he was not sure broadcasting the speech was a good idea. Apparently, some of his advisers were worried that Reagan's comments about problems with the Social Security system would scare away many older voters, undoing all of the work Goldwater and his staff had done to assure them that he did not want to eliminate Social Security. The advisers wanted to show a tape of Goldwater's meeting with former President Dwight D. Eisenhower instead.

What Reagan had said about Social Security was that he strongly supported it, but that the system needed to be fixed so that it would have the solid financial foundation it needed in order to be able to provide future benefits.

Reagan told Goldwater that he had been saying the same thing for weeks, and his comments had been very well received, but regardless, the decision on whether or not to air the speech was up to the group that had purchased the airtime. Goldwater told Reagan he had not actually heard the speech and that he would listen to a tape of it before making any decisions. Reagan thought that was fair. True to his word, Goldwater listened to the tape and called Reagan back to say he found nothing troubling about what had been said, and that it was okay to broadcast the speech as planned.

By this time, however, Reagan was having second thoughts. Maybe Goldwater's advisers were right and it was safer to show the film of Ike. Reagan thought about calling the group of donors and asking them to cancel the broadcast of his speech, but after a good night's sleep, he decided to proceed as planned.

His decision turned out to be the right course of action. A few hours after the broadcast, a Goldwater aide called Reagan to tell him the campaign headquarters switchboard had been flooded with calls from people wanting to help the campaign. Barry Goldwater was the man of the moment, but a new political star was born.

Ronald Reagan at an event supporting Goldwater's run for the presidency, 1964.

Chapter Three

THE GOVERNOR

Rendezvous
with Destiny

Though he was genuinely interested in national affairs and one of the country's most articulate and effective spokesmen on the issues of the day, it never occurred to Ronald Reagan that he should seek political office. As a movie star, and later a television personality, he was comfortable in front of the camera. While he derived great satisfaction from pleasing his audiences, the idea of raising money and waging a campaign asking people to vote for him so he could wield political power over them was not particularly appealing. It just was not how he saw himself. Besides, he was very happily married, enjoyed being a father, had a comfortable lifestyle that allowed him to be in control of his schedule, and though he was well known, still had relative privacy. Why would he want to disrupt that?

Fortunately, not everyone in California was as content to let Ronald Reagan be as he was. He had campaigned vigorously for Republican nominee Barry Goldwater in the 1964 presidential election, and although Goldwater was defeated by President Lyndon B. Johnson, Ronald Reagan's political career

Ronald Reagan at a media event, 1967.

was just beginning. The nationally televised speech he made on Goldwater's behalf had exhilarated the Republican Party, especially in California. Formally titled "A Time for Choosing," it came to be known as the "Rendezvous with Destiny" speech. It put Ronald Reagan on the political map. The words with which he closed that speech resonated far beyond the election at hand:

They say the world has become too complex for simple answers. They are wrong. . . . You and I have a rendezvous with destiny. We will preserve for our children this, the last, best hope of man on earth, or we will sentence them to take the last step into a thousand years of darkness.

We will keep in mind and remember that Barry Goldwater has faith in us. He has faith that you and I have the ability and the dignity and the right to make our own decisions and determine our own destiny.

After the election, Ronald Reagan went back to his job on *Death Valley Days* and continued to make speeches. Life was good. In the spring of 1965, Ronald Reagan received a telephone call that would change his life forever.

Holmes Tuttle, a wealthy car dealer, one of several major contributors with whom he had met the previous year after the political speech at the Coconut Grove, and one of the sponsors of the "Rendezvous with Destiny" speech broadcast, asked if he could come see Ronald Reagan at his home in Pacific Palisades. Tuttle and a few friends were welcomed warmly, but when they explained why they had come, they got anything but the desired reaction.

They wanted Ronald Reagan to run for governor of California in 1966 against incumbent Pat Brown. Reagan laughed, and politely but firmly told them he was not interested—at all. The group remained resolute in claiming that he was the only one who could defeat incumbent Governor Edmund G. "Pat" Brown and unite the California Republican Party, which had become quite divided following the Goldwater defeat. For Reagan, the idea was nonnegotiable.

Undeterred, Tuttle and his friends, along with other Republican groups, kept pressuring Reagan. For months his answer was no. For months they kept trying. Eventually, their persistence began to pay off. As much as he did not want to

become a politician, Ronald Reagan came to the conclusion that if those pleading with him were right, and his refusal to run contributed to making things worse for the state of California and for the Republican Party, he could not live with himself. Nancy agreed. So Reagan came up with what he thought was a compromise that he was confident would ultimately get him off the hook. He would spend six months making speeches throughout California, and then decide if he shared their view that only he could be the winning candidate. He fully expected he would find several other people who could fill the bill.

He was wrong. At speech after speech, audience members would urge him to run for governor. At the end of six months, it was clear that Holmes Tuttle and his colleagues were right, and Ronald Reagan was convinced. He announced his candidacy on January 4, 1966.

The Reagans during the gubernatorial campaign, East Los Angeles, 1966. **Pages 92–93:** A Reagan campaign poster for governor, 1966.

Ronald Reagan at a campaign fund-raising event during his race
for governor, Hollywood, 1966.

"Reagan Girls" with signature sheets at the Republican headquarters, 1966.

The Republican primary campaign to choose the party's nominee was marked by vicious personal attacks against Reagan from his opponent, San Francisco Mayor George Christopher. Voters wanted no part of the negative campaigning, and handed Reagan his first political victory. Now it was time for Reagan to take on Governor Brown.

Brown, who had previously defeated Richard Nixon, was certain he would be elected to a third term. He mounted a nasty campaign against Reagan, making fun of his background as an actor. He even tried to smear Reagan by running a commercial that pointed out that an actor—John Wilkes Booth—had assassinated Abraham Lincoln.

Despite the mean-spirited assault from the opposition, Ronald Reagan would not take the bait. He conducted a campaign that was positive and focused on the issues. He told the people what he believed and why he wanted to be their governor. He took questions from audiences everywhere he went, and they felt a personal rapport with him.

Reagan won in a landslide, by a margin of almost one million votes, carrying all but three counties in the state. By his own admission, Reagan was neither a politician nor an experienced government manager. Maybe that's why the people elected him. Regardless, he was on his way to Sacramento to govern. Expectations were high.

He devoted himself to learning everything he could about the myriad of problems facing the state. Reagan knew that nothing was more important than personnel decisions. He believed in setting clear priorities, finding the best people possible, and letting them do their jobs. To that end, he specifically sought people who did not necessarily want jobs in government, but who would be willing to come with him to Sacramento because they shared his vision and believed in serving the people. Many came from the private sector for far less pay than they had been earning. Ultimately, the men and women who would compose the Reagan administration would be the architects of its success—for this term and for years to come.

Ronald and Nancy Reagan celebrate Reagan's election as governor at the Biltmore Hotel in Los Angeles, 1966. **Page 99:** The Reagan family, circa 1966.

Those who came to this untamed
land brought family. And family
built a nation. I'm convinced today
that the majority of Americans
want what those first Americans
wanted: A better life for themselves
and their children, a minimum
of government authority.

———

Ronald Reagan,
national television address,
July 6, 1976

A Voice for California

When he took office on January 3, 1967, California's thirty-third governor found his state in worse financial shape than he had originally thought. The deficit was at least $200 million. Fixing that was his first priority, but it would not be easy. Tough decisions would have to be made. Reagan was prepared to make them, and he spoke honestly with the people of California about what lay ahead. His path was more challenging because Democrats controlled the state legislature and were disinclined to let a Republican governor run the show. The new governor had campaigned on certain promises. He saw himself as having been sent to Sacramento by the people, who expected him to keep those promises.

Early on, with no other way to close the budget gap he inherited, Governor Reagan reluctantly allowed a short-term tax increase. He also imposed a budget cut and froze government

Ronald Reagan being sworn in as governor of California, 1967.

hiring. Both helped put the state's finances back on track. In fact, the next year California projected a budget surplus of more than $100 million for the following fiscal year.

By virtue of being governor of California, Ronald Reagan became a national Republican figure, and some party activists thought of him as a potential presidential candidate in 1968. Ronald Reagan, however, was not among them. When Republican officials asked him to run as a "favorite son" in the California primary to help avoid a messy fight between candidates Richard Nixon, Nelson Rockefeller, and George Romney, Reagan said "no." But the officials persisted, pointing out that winning the primary as a favorite son meant only that a battle would be avoided and the governor would be the leader of the state's delegation to the Republican National Convention in Miami Beach in August.

Reagan agreed, but on one condition. California's slate of delegates had to be balanced fairly to represent all factions in the party, not just one. State party officials agreed, Reagan's name was placed on the ballot, and he "won" the primary. As a result, his name would be placed in nomination at the convention, but to Reagan, that was only a formality of being the favorite son. He did not consider himself a "real" candidate, and said so to anyone who asked. Nonetheless, a few diehards worked against the governor's wishes to rally support for him at the convention. While he ultimately got more votes than expected, when it was clear that Nixon was the favorite, Governor Reagan took to the podium to ask the delegates to nominate Nixon by acclamation, which they did. After the convention, the Reagans went on a short cruise in the Florida Keys, giving not a moment's thought to what had happened in Miami Beach. So much for that "Reagan for President" campaign.

As usual, the governor was happy to return home to California, even though a full plate awaited him in Sacramento. Finances were not the only turmoil facing the state. California had become a hotbed of antiwar and other protests, some of which had spun out of control into violent situations. The volatility at the University of California at

Berkeley was especially dangerous. In less than a year, there had been several bombings and attempted bombings on campus. Hundreds of weapons had been confiscated, including dynamite and Molotov cocktails. In the spring of 1969, things turned ugly when thousands of protestors charged a line of police in Berkeley, injuring scores of people. The situation was escalating, and the governor had to act.

While he was a fervent believer in the constitutionally protected rights to free speech and assembly, Governor Reagan did not believe those freedoms included the right to incite violence. At the request of the university president, the mayor, and the local police chief, he sent in the National Guard to restore order so the university could get back to the business of educating its students, and the surrounding community could return to its safe, peaceful existence. His decision was not without controversy, but the problem was solved.

As 1969 came to an end, it was clear to Governor Reagan that he had not completed his work. Even though some special elections had resulted in a Republican legislature, allowing the governor to pass dozens of anticrime bills, there were still important goals to accomplish; chief among them was welfare reform. He decided to seek a second—and last—term as California's chief executive.

Running against California's speaker of the assembly and his fierce political opponent, Jesse Unruh, Governor Reagan swept to victory with 53 percent of the vote. He viewed that as a mandate to, in his words, "keep on keepin' on" in terms of the reforms he began in his first term.

The centerpiece of Governor Reagan's second term was welfare reform. He believed deeply that the government should help those in need who could not help themselves, such as the impoverished, elderly, blind, and disabled. It was well-known that California's welfare rolls had become bloated. In fact, between 1960 and 1970, the number of people receiving welfare checks had almost quadrupled to a number exceeding a staggering two million.

Page 104: Ronald Reagan delivering a speech, 1970.

Those nations and states
which have secured man's
highest aspirations for freedom,
opportunity, and justice have
always been those willing
to trust their people, confident
that their skills and their talents
are equal to any challenge.

———

Ronald Reagan,
address as governor of California,
1974

It was critical to reduce that number without hurting those in need. An important goal of reform was to break the cycle whereby generation after generation of a family ended up on welfare. Governor Reagan believed that this would not only save the state a significant amount of money, but would also help people develop the self-confidence and dignity that came from being able to support themselves.

Resisting pressure from one side to virtually eliminate welfare altogether, and from the other side to impose a huge tax increase to fund the system, the Reagan administration crafted a plan to tighten eligibility rules so that only the truly needy would receive public assistance, and wasteful spending would be eliminated. The governor knew that passage of his program would not be easy. So he went straight to the one group whose pressure could make the legislature act—the people.

In campaignlike mode, Governor Reagan made speech after speech all over the state, explaining what was in his reform plan and urging the people to tell their representatives to support it. Pro–welfare reform committees were organized and mobilized in all of California's fifty-eight counties. The campaign succeeded. The Democratic speaker of the state assembly came to see the governor, and relented.

Joined by staffers, the two leaders sat down together and in little more than a week hammered out a welfare reform proposal that not only wound up saving California's taxpayers hundreds of millions of dollars, but also raised the benefits and provided cost-of-living increases for those truly in need. The Welfare Reform Act was signed into law in August 1971.

Governor Reagan's second term also brought a fourth rebate of state taxes to Californians, something of which he was especially proud. Over his eight years in office, largely through property-tax relief, the Reagan administration gave back more than $5 billion to the taxpayers. The governor always viewed that money as the people's to begin with, and the way he saw it, he was just returning what had been borrowed to its rightful owners.

Due to of the size of its economy and the vast number of exports and imports crossing its borders, California had, and still maintains today, important relations with countries around the world. That gave the governor an opportunity to establish relationships with foreign leaders, something that would serve him well later. Not only did the Reagans regularly host world leaders visiting California, they also, at the behest of President Nixon, went overseas four times on goodwill missions to Europe and Asia. In addition to meeting with heads of state to convey personal messages from Nixon, Governor Reagan always found time to promote California's businesses on those trips.

Despite the urgings of many supporters and friends, Governor Reagan kept his word that his second term would be his last. He had accomplished most of what he wanted to do, and believed it should be someone else's turn. But he did admit that although he had been initially reluctant to run for office, being governor made "everything else we've ever done seem as dull as dishwater."

President Gerald R. Ford offered the outgoing governor positions in his cabinet and the post of ambassador to the Court of St. James, but Reagan politely declined. He respected the president, of course, and was flattered by the offers, but, as would become clear soon, being part of the Ford administration was not how he envisioned the next chapter of his career.

Though not in office, Reagan intended to be visible and active on the national political scene, making speeches, campaigning for Republican candidates, writing columns, offering commentary on the radio, and doing whatever else he could to advance the causes in which he believed. His longtime aides Michael Deaver and Peter Hannaford established a public relations firm to handle what would be a deluge of invitations and opportunities for the popular ex-governor.

He and Nancy wanted to take a step back—at least for a little while—from the hectic pace and glare of public life they had been living with for the past eight years. They were eagerly looking forward to spending more time with family and friends in Los Angeles, and especially wanted to enjoy their newly purchased ranch high in the Santa Ynez mountains just north of Santa Barbara. Originally called Tip Top, the Reagans renamed the 688-acre property Rancho del Cielo—Ranch in the Sky.

Pages 108–109: Ronald Reagan with his horses, Rancho del Cielo, 1976.

From some points on the ranch,
you can watch boats cruising
across the Santa Barbara
Channel, then turn your head
and see the Santa Ynez Valley
unfold like a huge wilderness
amphitheater before your eyes.

———

Ronald Reagan,
from An American Life

Rancho del Cielo captivated the Reagans from the moment they saw it. It came with a modest plastered adobe house desperately in need of repairs, but a small lake and a stable for horses made it perfect. It was like no other place they had seen, and its new owner described it in vivid, almost magical terms.

"From the first day we saw it," Reagan later reminisced, "Rancho del Cielo cast a spell over us. No place before or since has given Nancy and me the joy and serenity it does." Blessed with a large meadow crowned with oak trees, the ranch was expansive, both in size and in the breadth of its natural beauty. Mountains stretched toward the horizon and, in the distance, one could make out sunlight glinting on the Santa Barbara Channel and the Santa Ynez Valley that, in Reagan's words, unfurled itself like a "huge wilderness amphiteater" across the land. A source of solace during times of stress, the Reagans would call the ranch home for many years.

The Reagans spent a lot of time on the ranch after leaving Sacramento—riding horses, taking long walks, and paddling in their canoe. Sometimes the former governor would come to the ranch to work on repairs to the house and barn, while Mrs. Reagan would stay at their home in Pacific Palisades, spending time with family and friends and attending to charitable activities. But usually after a day or two, either he would come home or she would go to the ranch. They did not like being apart for long.

Life was good for the Reagans in 1975. They had nearly everything they wanted: good health, beautiful homes, family and friends, and freedom. The former governor was a respected voice on national issues and very much in demand on the speaking circuit. Many saw him as the Republican Party's most popular leader, notwithstanding the fact that there was a Republican president in the White House. Hardly a day went by when he did not receive calls and letters from across the country, urging him to run for president.

Content as he was with his post-gubernatorial life, Ronald Reagan was concerned about the direction in which the country was headed. Despite his respect for Gerald Ford, and deep reservations about challenging an incumbent president of his

own party, as the year went on, Ronald Reagan heard more and more from his party leaders that he was needed in Washington. Unlike when he was first approached to run for governor, he was not resistant to the idea of seeking political office now, and it was clear that the people wanted him. He and Nancy talked it over and agreed that he had to run. On November 20, 1975, Ronald Reagan announced that he was seeking the Republican nomination for president of the United States.

Ronald Reagan, campaigning for president, 1976.

Ronald Reagan during a campaign speech in California, 1966.

Governor Ronald Reagan throwing out the first pitch at Anaheim Stadium, California, 1966.

Governor Ronald Reagan speaking at a swearing-in ceremony, Sacramento, California, 1967.

Governor Reagan speaking at the Inaugural Ball, California State Fairgrounds, Sacramento, California, 1967.

Governor Reagan on *Face the Nation*, circa 1968. **Opposite, top:** The Reagans and the Nixons at the Rose Bowl Game, Pasadena, California, 1969. **Opposite, bottom:** Governor Reagan giving a speech at Loma Linda University to announce the building of a new VA hospital, 1971. President Richard Nixon is seated to his right. **Page 118:** The Reagans on the campaign trail, circa 1970.

Millions of Americans, especially
our own sons and daughters, are seeking
for a cause they can believe in. There is
a hunger in this country today—a hunger
for spiritual guidance. People yearn
once again to be proud of their country
and proud of themselves, and to have
confidence in themselves. And there's
every reason why they should be proud.

———

Ronald Reagan,
remarks at the Convention of Southern GOP,
Atlanta, Georgia, December 7, 1973

The Great Communicator

Ronald Reagan's candidacy electrified the Republican Party. He ran a vigorous national campaign, drawing huge crowds everywhere he went. Against daunting odds, candidate Reagan won several key primaries and came within seventy votes of being the party's nominee. After Ford's acceptance speech, Ronald Reagan joined him on the convention podium and, in a moment that brought both tears and wild applause, pledged his full support to the Ford–Dole ticket.

No one who had seen the enthusiastic reception that the delegates gave Ronald Reagan when he appeared on stage at the 1976 Republican National Convention doubted that Reagan would be a candidate again in 1980. Most expected him to be on the circuit again that year—as the party's nominee. Disappointed though they had been, the Reagans had no regrets about the 1976 campaign and did not look back after the convention, only forward.

Ronald Reagan campaigned tirelessly for Ford and Republican candidates in dozens of states, but when all the

Ronald Reagan on the presidential campaign trail greeting supporters, 1976.

votes were counted, America had a new president—Georgia Governor Jimmy Carter.

Ronald Reagan continued writing his newspaper column, making speeches, and, of course, spending time at the ranch with Nancy. Mrs. Reagan kept busy with the Foster Grandparents Program and other charitable activities in the Los Angeles area. They socialized often with friends and enjoyed family gatherings for birthdays and holidays. The Reagans traveled abroad a few times, including to London, where they ran into a friend from Los Angeles, who arranged a meeting for Reagan with the recently elected head of Britain's Conservative Party, Margaret Thatcher. They liked each other immediately, and what was supposed to be a five-minute meet-and-greet turned into almost two hours of conversation about reducing government spending. It was the start of a lifelong relationship neither could have possibly imagined.

Back home, while indisputably the party favorite, Ronald Reagan's path to the 1980 nomination was not without a potential bump or two. Foremost was the issue of his age. Were he to be elected, Ronald Reagan would be the oldest president in U.S. history. He had never felt better and his energy level had never been higher, but he knew there would be some concern about his age. The only way to counter that concern was to run a vigorous campaign and show people he had the stamina the job required. To the dismay of his aides, that often meant campaigning from early in the morning to late at night. But the long hours didn't seem to tire the candidate. In fact, often when the entourage was back on the campaign plane en route to the next stop, everyone, including staffers half the candidate's age, napped except for one person—Ronald Reagan. Many times, other than the pilots and flight attendants, he was the only person awake on the plane. Nancy was usually curled up next to him while he read newspapers and memos or worked on a speech.

Another bump was the multitude of other candidates in the race. Longtime Republican stalwart George H. W. Bush; former Texas governor, Treasury secretary, and Democrat-turned-Republican John Connally; Senator Howard Baker of Watergate Committee fame; conservative Congressman Phil Crane; and 1976 Republican vice presidential candidate Senator Bob Dole were among those also seeking the nomination.

Nonetheless, when he formally declared his candidacy on November 20, 1979, most expected Reagan to have little difficulty in wrapping up the nomination early. They were not disappointed. After a decisive victory in New Hampshire in February, the campaigns of most of the other candidates soon ended. Only George H. W. Bush remained in the race, but he quit in May. The nomination was Ronald Reagan's, and attention turned to whom he would choose as a running mate.

In the weeks leading up to the convention, there had been some rumblings about former President Gerald Ford joining the ticket with his former rival, in what some described as a "dream ticket" of Republican unity. Nominee-in-waiting Reagan initially liked the idea, and when he arrived in Detroit for his party's convention in July, he hoped things could be worked out. Talk of a Reagan–Ford ticket was rampant, reaching almost a fever pitch among delegates and journalists. Aides to both men met to structure a power-sharing arrangement, but there were significant disagreements.

While these meetings were going on, Ford gave a television interview in which he outlined the terms under which he would be willing to join Reagan on the ticket. Essentially, he wanted to be a co-president. Reagan saw the interview and was beginning to have misgivings about the idea, but was still willing to see if a deal could be struck. It could not. Shortly after that interview, Ford took himself out of consideration.

After conferring with Nancy and a small group of aides, Reagan decided to ask George H. W. Bush to be his running mate. Reagan had always respected Bush, and felt he was the most qualified to step into the presidency if the need ever arose. Not only that, Bush was also well-regarded in the party and an experienced campaigner. The call was made, and the offer accepted.

Page 124: Reagan on the presidential campaign trail, 1979.

Someone once said that the difference
between an American and any other
kind of person is that an American lives
in anticipation of the future because
he knows it will be a great place. Other
people fear the future as just a repetition
of past failures. There's a lot of truth in
that. If there is one thing we are sure of
it is that history need not be relived; that
nothing is impossible, and that man is
capable of improving his circumstances
beyond what we are told is fact.

———

Ronald Reagan,
announcing his bid for the presidency,
New York Hilton, NY, November 13, 1979

On July 17, 1980, Ronald Reagan stood exactly where his supporters had been waiting for him to stand for four years—at the podium of the Republican National Convention as the party's nominee for the presidency of the United States. In a stirring speech that took the Carter administration to task for its failures, Reagan offered an optimistic, uplifting view of America and why he wanted to be president:

More than anything else, I want my candidacy to unify our country; to renew the American spirit and sense of purpose. I want to carry our message to every American, regardless of party affiliation, who is a member of this community of shared values.

. . . I will not stand by and watch this great country destroy itself under mediocre leadership that drifts from one crisis to the next, eroding our national will and purpose. We have come together here because the American people deserve better from those to whom they entrust our nation's highest offices, and we stand united in our resolve to do something about it.

. . . Together, let us make this a new beginning. Let us make a commitment to care for the needy; to teach our children the values and the virtues handed down to us by our families; to have the courage to defend those values and the willingness to sacrifice for them.

. . . Let us pledge to restore, in our time, the American spirit of voluntary service, of cooperation, of private and community initiative, a spirit that flows like a deep and mighty river through the history of our nation.

Ronald Reagan and George H. W. Bush were ready to take on Jimmy Carter and Walter Mondale.

The Reagan campaign maintained a careful balance between pointing out the shortcomings of the Carter presidency by outlining specific solutions to the myriad of problems the country faced, and providing an inspiring and positive vision of what a new administration could mean for the country. The polls were encouraging, but the candidate and his team knew that to seal the deal with the American people, it was essential for him to cross the threshold of perception. Voters needed to be able to see Ronald Reagan as the president. The way to do that was a side-by-side comparison with Carter. A debate was essential, but Carter was resistant.

Ultimately, Reagan participated in two debates during the general election campaign. The first one was in September with Congressman John Anderson, a Republican who was running as an independent candidate. Carter declined to participate in that debate. Under intense public pressure, Carter finally agreed to one debate with his Republican opponent. At the end of October in Cleveland, Reagan and Carter had their only face-to-face confrontation of the campaign. It was obvious why Reagan was known as the Great Communicator. Carter answered questions with the demeanor of the nuclear engineer he was. Reagan, on the other hand, answered questions with confidence and optimism. He even managed to get in a memorable zinger, shaking his head and saying to Carter, "There you go again," when he falsely accused Reagan of being opposed to Social Security and Medicare. Reagan's closing statement was memorable. He urged voters to ask themselves a question when deciding for whom to cast their ballots: Were they better off than they were four years ago? If yes, Reagan said they should vote for Carter. But if they were not, Reagan asked them to vote for him and the changes he would bring to Washington.

Any chance Carter had of being reelected vanished that night. The polls showed a steady rise in voter support for the Reagan–Bush ticket, but the candidate took nothing for granted, campaigning hard until the very end. On Election Day, he and Nancy voted at their usual polling place near their Pacific Palisades home, and spent most of the day there. Late in the afternoon, they started to get ready to go to the home of their friends Earle and Marion Jorgensen to follow their election night tradition of dining with a small group of close friends while awaiting the returns.

The candidate was in the shower when the phone rang, and he did not hear it. Nancy, who had already taken her bath, answered and shouted for her husband to come out for a call. "It's Jimmy Carter," she said. Ronald Reagan stepped out of the shower, wrapped a towel around himself, and picked up the phone in their bathroom. With Nancy at his side and still dripping wet, he said hello and confirmed that he was, in fact, Ronald Reagan.

The White House operator announced that the president was calling and a split second later, Jimmy Carter was on the line. In his familiar Southern drawl, he conceded the election and congratulated Ronald Wilson Reagan on being elected the fortieth president of the United States. The president-elect thanked him and hung up the phone. With tears in their eyes, Nancy and Ronald Reagan looked at each other and embraced.

Then, like any other election night, they dressed for dinner and went to the Jorgensens' house. But this was not just any other election night. Even before they walked out their front door, it was apparent that everything had changed. Additional Secret Service agents hovered nearby, cars had been added to their motorcade, large crowds gathered along their route, and TV cameras recorded their every move.

After dinner, the president-elect and Nancy went to the Century Plaza Hotel to thank their supporters. Reagan spoke confidently of the future, saying, "I am not frightened by what lies ahead, and I don't believe the American people are frightened by what lies ahead. Together, we're going to do what has to be done."

The next morning he held a press conference, and then set about the business of choosing a cabinet and senior team that would help him fulfill the promise his election represented. The future was now at hand.

Ronald Reagan signing "America–Reagan Country" campaign posters, 1980.

The Reagans greeting supporters, 1980.

The newly inaugurated fortieth president of the United States
Ronald Reagan with Nancy Reagan during the inaugural parade,
1981.

Chapter Four

THE PRESIDENT

A Voice for America

Ronald Reagan made a point of saying that one does not "become" president. Rather, the president is "given temporary custody of this great institution which was created by our Founding Fathers."

When "custodian" Ronald Reagan took the oath of office as America's fortieth president on January 20, 1981, the country was experiencing one of its bleakest economic times since the Great Depression. Taxes, unemployment, and interest rates were high, and the national morale was low.

Restoring America's economic health was the new president's top priority. He shared his vision in his first inaugural address:

This administration's objective will be a healthy, vigorous, growing economy that provides equal opportunities for all Americans, with no barriers born of bigotry or discrimination. Putting America back to work means putting all Americans back to work. Ending inflation means freeing all Americans from the terror of runaway living costs. All must share in the productive work of this "new beginning," and all must share in the bounty of a revived economy.

President Reagan broke tradition by holding his inaugural ceremony on the west side of the Capitol so he would face his beloved state of California, 1981.

President Reagan had earned a degree in economics at Eureka College, and even though he would sometimes joke about "two economists having three opinions," he knew what needed to be done and how to do it. He had a simple but specific plan of which he had spoken often during the campaign: Cut taxes, get control of federal spending, and get the government out of the way so that the entrepreneurial spirit of the American people could be unleashed. Some skeptics derisively called his plan "Reaganomics," but President Reagan was undeterred. He knew that if people had money in their pockets and incentives to invest and build businesses, jobs would be created, inflation tamed, and interest rates reduced.

As soon as the inaugural ceremony was over, President Reagan set his sights on Capitol Hill. From day one, he and his team worked tirelessly to get Congress to pass legislation to put the economy back on track.

He nearly lost his chance when on March 30, 1981, he was shot and seriously wounded in an assassination attempt. As he was getting into his car after giving a speech at a Washington hotel, a bullet ricocheted off his limousine door and lodged perilously close to his heart. Secret Service agents practically threw him into the presidential limousine and took off for the White House. On the ride over, he had trouble breathing and was coughing up blood, so they diverted him to the George Washington University Hospital's emergency room.

By the time the motorcade arrived at the hospital, President Reagan was weak and nearly collapsed as he tried to walk from his car to the emergency room door. He was immediately placed on a gurney, where doctors and nurses began to work on him. Drifting in and out of consciousness, he looked up and saw Nancy. In a barely audible voice he said, "Honey, I forgot to duck," and was whisked into surgery while Nancy waited nearby. With her was Sarah Brady, wife of Press Secretary Jim Brady, who had taken a bullet in his head and whose survival was very much in doubt. Brady had also

President Reagan holding a senior staff meeting with Mike Deaver, James Baker, and Ed Meese on his first official day back in the Oval Office after recovering from the assassination attempt, 1981.

been taken to the George Washington University Hospital by ambulance shortly after the president.

The president survived the surgery, but developed an infection in the days following and came very close to dying. Brady, too, survived surgery but emerged with severe brain damage, leaving him unable to care for himself and with reduced cognitive skills. Despite the fact that Brady could not actually perform the duties of the president's press secretary, Reagan decided Brady would keep that title for the remainder of his presidency.

Even an assassination attempt did not slow the new president down. While still recovering, he summoned congressional leaders to the White House to press his support for his economic recovery proposals. Ronald Reagan may have been the first president to wear pajamas to a meeting with the bipartisan congressional leadership. He wanted them to know he meant business.

His efforts paid off. In August, President Reagan signed the Economic Recovery Tax Act of 1981, which brought reductions in individual income tax rates, the expensing of depreciable property, and incentives for small businesses and for savings. So began the Reagan Recovery. A few years later, the Tax Reform Act of 1986 brought the lowest individual and corporate income tax rates of any major industrialized country in the world.

The numbers tell the story. Over the eight years of the Reagan administration:

- Twenty million new jobs were created;
- Inflation dropped from 13.5 percent in 1980 to 4.1 percent in 1988;
- Unemployment fell from 7.6 percent to 5.5 percent;
- The net worth of families earning between $20,000 and $50,000 annually grew by 27 percent;
- The real Gross National Product rose 26 percent;
- The prime interest rate was slashed by more than half, from 21.5 percent in January 1981 to 10 percent in August 1988.

Given actual rates of inflation, through 1987, the Reagan tax cuts saved the median-income, two-earner American family of four close to $9,000 in taxes from what it would have owed in 1980.

Tax cuts were only one "leg of the stool." The second was job creation. Millions of new jobs were created, and as President Reagan had pledged in his inaugural address, they were not limited to just one segment of society. Employment of African Americans rose by more than 25 percent between 1982 and 1988, and more than half of the new jobs created were filled by women.

Taming the lion of government spending was another key component of the plan—the third leg of the stool. Here, too, President Reagan did what he said he would do. During his administration, growth in government spending plummeted from 10 percent in 1982 to just over 1 percent in 1987. With inflation factored in, federal spending actually declined in 1987—the first time that had happened in over a decade.

So impressive was the Reagan Recovery that at the 1983 G-7 Economic Summit, when it was obvious the president's plan was working, the West German chancellor asked him to "tell us about the American miracle." That was quite a turnaround from two years earlier, when President Reagan outlined his economic recovery plan to a group of skeptical world leaders. Now, however, they all wanted to know how he did it, so he told them: Reducing tax rates restored the incentive to produce and create jobs, and getting the government out of the way allowed people to become entrepreneurs. From there, the free marketplace operated as it should.

As President Reagan observed with a wry smile, "I could tell our economic program was working when they stopped calling it Reaganomics." What pleased him most about the Reagan Recovery was not the vindication or all the impressive statistics. To him, the success of Reaganomics was what it brought to the American people. Millions had good jobs and were able to keep more of the money for which they worked so hard. Families could reliably plan a budget and pay their bills. The seemingly insatiable federal government was on a much-needed diet. Businesses and individual entrepreneurs were no longer hassled by the government, or paralyzed by burdensome and unnecessary regulations every time they wanted to expand.

Achieving the American dream was possible once again.

Ronald Reagan is sworn in as president by Chief Justice Warren Burger, 1981. **Opposite:** Outgoing U.S. President Jimmy Carter sits with president-elect Ronald Reagan en route to Reagan's presidential inauguration ceremony, 1981. **Pages 140–141:** The Reagans attend a dinner at the Grand Trianon Palace in Versailles, France, during the annual economic summit, 1982. **Pages 144–145:** President and Mrs. Reagan welcome Mother Teresa of Calcutta to the White House to honor her charitable works, 1981.

It is up to us, however we
may disagree on policies,
to work together for progress
and humanity so that our
grandchildren, when they look
back on us, can say we not only
preserved the flame of freedom,
but cast its warmth and light
further than those
who came before us.

———

Ronald Reagan,
remarks to the National Conference
of Christians and Jews,
New York, NY, March 23, 1981

President Reagan meeting with the press after signing the
Economic Recovery Tax Act of 1981 at Rancho del Cielo.

President Reagan showing off a whimsical drawing to the White House staff photographer, 1981.

President Reagan and Vice President Bush receiving a briefing in
the Situation Room on the assassination of President Anwar Sadat
of the Arab Republic of Egypt, 1981.

President Reagan, Jimmy Carter, Rosalynn Carter, Nancy Reagan, Gerald Ford, and Richard Nixon, 1981.

Economic Strategist

Given the dire state of the economy facing Ronald Reagan when he assumed the presidency, it would have been understandable had he focused exclusively on economic challenges. But there were many important problems to solve.

Getting the economy back on track was only one part of the story. President Reagan had sworn to uphold the Constitution and he took seriously his obligation to "form a more perfect union, establish justice, insure domestic tranquility, provide for the common defense, [and] promote the general welfare." He came to office with a mandate to address a broad array of important domestic issues, and he did.

One issue of particular importance to the president was how well the government served the people. He firmly believed that the government should work for the people, not the other way around. President Reagan thought of the people as his boss—by electing him, they had hired him to do a job on their behalf. Throughout his political career, Ronald Reagan was fond of telling true stories about the illogical and often

As the first commander in chief to routinely do so, President Reagan returns a salute to a marine after landing with Mrs. Reagan on the White House South Lawn, 1982.

mind-boggling—not to mention exasperating—inefficiency of the federal bureaucracy. Although he did so with a smile, underlying the storytelling was a deep frustration. He vowed that if he ever had an opportunity to do something about it, he would. And he did. Not only did his administration reduce the burden of excessive, redundant, and unnecessary paperwork on businesses working with the government, it made changes that affected real people on a daily basis. When President Reagan took office, it took seven weeks to get a Social Security card and forty-three days to get a passport. By the time he left, either one—or both—could be obtained in just ten days.

As much as he used his own passport over the years, and as unique and exciting as some of his foreign trips were, Ronald Reagan always looked forward to coming home. He genuinely loved America. From his beloved California to the New York island, he was in awe of the country's sheer physical beauty. "Spacious skies, amber waves of grain, purple mountains' majesties, and oceans white with foam" were not just words to him. It was how he saw America. He believed he had a special responsibility to protect the country's environment and to preserve its natural beauty. President Reagan did more than just talk about it. The Reagan administration was the first to establish a special unit at the Department of Justice to prosecute criminal polluters.

Polluters were not the only criminals President Reagan intended to put out of business. Safety was always a top-of-agenda item for the Reagan administration. It took a while, but in 1984, Congress passed the president's Comprehensive Crime Control Act, which kept criminals behind bars, restricted the use of the insanity defense, reviewed federal sentencing guidelines, and toughened penalties for drug dealers and others. That same year, the president signed another significant piece of legislation, making child pornography a separate criminal offense. The effects of the president's work to reduce crime and put criminals where they belonged was dramatic. Nearly two million fewer households were hit by crime in 1987 than in 1980.

President Reagan reads a newspaper on the Truman Balcony of the White House, 1981.

President Reagan with James Baker, new Secretary of State-designate George Shultz, Bill Clark, and Ed Meese at Camp David, Maryland, 1982.

Signing ceremony in the East Room for The Voting Rights Act of 1982.

President Reagan, concerned over his father-in-law's failing health, speaks to Mrs. Reagan in Arizona from Camp David, Maryland, 1982. **Opposite, top:** President Reagan and Vice President Bush having lunch in White House, 1982. **Opposite, bottom:** President Reagan offering hands-on support for flood victims in devastated Monroe, Louisiana, 1983.

President Reagan reviews the troops as part of the
recommissioning ceremony for the battleship USS *New Jersey*
in Long Beach, California, 1982.

President and Mrs. Reagan talk to space shuttle astronauts Captain Mattingly and Colonel Hartsfield at Edwards Air Force Base just prior to their mission, 1982.

Defender of Justice

Advocating crime prevention and locking up criminals were only part of what President Reagan did to ensure liberty and justice for all. Another key component of his agenda was the appointment of judges who would faithfully interpret the Constitution rather than legislate from the bench. Of all the judicial appointments made by President Reagan, none was more historically significant than that of Sandra Day O'Connor in 1981. When he became the first president to nominate a woman to serve on the United States Supreme Court, it shattered a glass ceiling that had been in place since the founding of the country, forever changing not only the judiciary but the aspirations of women in our society. Little girls everywhere could now reach professional heights previously unavailable to them.

In many ways, President Reagan's nomination of Sandra Day O'Connor was emblematic of how he viewed people—without an iota of prejudice, just as Jack and Nelle had raised him. Gender, race, ethnicity, and religion just did not matter to him in the slightest. They were never factors in his decision making, other than when people were being discriminated against. When that

President Reagan and Sandra Day O'Connor after her swearing-in ceremony as the first woman justice of the U.S. Supreme Court, 1981.

happened, President Reagan was a tenacious fighter for equal rights. Under his leadership, the federal government equaled or surpassed the number of civil rights cases enforced by any previous administration in virtually every category. During the eight years of the Reagan administration, principal civil rights organizations received almost 18 percent more in funding.

President Reagan never forgot what it was like to grow up in a household with limited financial means. As such, he was genuinely concerned with helping the poor advance beyond poverty. He backed up his words with action: Under his leadership, federal spending for basic low-income assistance programs rose by 40 percent.

President Reagan understood, from personal experience, that a good education was the ticket out of poverty. When his National Commission on Excellence in Education termed the United States "A Nation at Risk" because of declining educational quality, the president called for a variety of remedies, including overall higher standards and accountability as well as merit pay for teachers and principals. As critical as those measures were, America's long-term well-being and its ability to compete in an increasingly global marketplace required more than excellence in education. It required looking beyond our shores.

To help maintain prosperity and domestic tranquility, President Reagan implemented a well-defined and realistic foreign policy, one that would not only preserve, but also strengthen America's leadership position in the world.

Doing that often meant "flying the flag" in foreign capitals. Truth be told, President Reagan was not exactly a fan of airplane travel—especially if it meant to faraway places without Nancy. Once when talking to an aide about upcoming foreign travel and the number of flights required, the president said, "The highest I want to go is on the saddle of a horse." Yet he understood the importance of representing America abroad and of forming relationships with his counterparts, and he climbed the steps of Air Force One many times over the eight years, visiting more than two dozen countries and traveling more than 660,000 miles. When he stood in a foreign capital and heard "The Star-

Spangled Banner" played by the host country's band, President Reagan seemed to stand just a little taller and his chest swelled ever so slightly. His pride in representing the United States was almost palpable.

He believed fervently in the greatness and goodness of America, and knew that American strength and stability was central to world peace. One of his first priorities as president was taking a demoralized and underfunded U.S. military and giving it the support and resources it needed to keep America safe and be a force for peace around the globe. Nothing made him prouder than to be commander in chief. His face expressed how much it meant to receive—and return—a salute. He felt a special bond with the men and women in uniform, especially the young people from the small towns across America. That they were willing to risk their lives for their country never ceased to amaze and humble President Reagan. He took no responsibility more seriously than to try to keep them out of harm's way. He made a commitment to them that if it ever became necessary to send them into battle, he would make sure they had what they needed to successfully get the job done. By the time President Reagan left office, the U.S. military budget had increased 43 percent over what it had been during the height of the Vietnam War. Troop levels increased; weapons and equipment were improved, vastly.

Ronald Reagan strengthened the military because he was a realist. He understood the world, and had a clear sense of what America's role in it should be—the champion of freedom for people everywhere.

President and Mrs. Reagan welcoming Queen Elizabeth II and Prince Philip of Great Britain with a formal arrival ceremony, Santa Barbara, California, 1983.

President Reagan speaking to U.S. troops at the DMZ during his trip to the Republic of Korea, 1983.

President and Mrs. Reagan enjoying a moment together on the
shore of Lake Lucky at Rancho del Cielo, 1983.

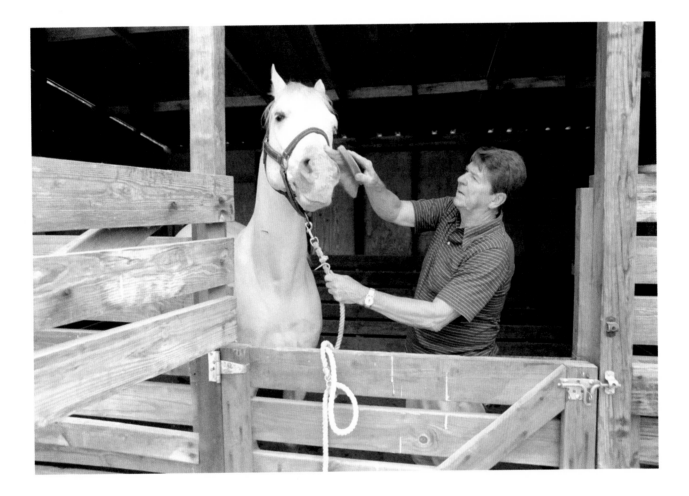

President Reagan grooming El Alamein at Rancho del Cielo, 1983.

A Champion for World Peace

Perhaps his most steadfast ally in the pursuit of global freedom was British Prime Minister Margaret Thatcher. From the day they first met in London well before they were in office, the two just clicked. They saw the world in similar ways and found themselves in agreement on most global issues. The United States and Britain were said to have a special relationship, perhaps best evidenced by the fact that the Reagans' first state dinner in 1981 and last state dinner in 1988 were both in honor of Mrs. Thatcher.

The special relationship between the United States and the United Kingdom was not limited to the prime minister. Indeed, the Reagans and members of the British royal family came to be friends, so much so that Queen Elizabeth II invited President Reagan to go horseback riding with her at Windsor Castle and Mrs. Reagan was an honored guest at two royal weddings. While visiting California in 1983, Queen Elizabeth and Prince Philip even braved a severe rainstorm to travel up the Santa Ynez Mountain roads to visit the Reagans at their ranch.

President and Mrs. Reagan hosting Prime Minister Margaret Thatcher and Denis Thatcher at their last state dinner, 1988. **Page 172:** The Reagans attending a memorial service at Camp Lejeune, North Carolina, for servicemen killed in Lebanon and Grenada, 1983.

The friendship with the British royal family would continue for many years, even after the Reagans left the White House.

His Holiness Pope John Paul II was another leader with whom President Reagan had a special rapport. Their relationship went far beyond the usual ceremonial events between a president and a pope. As they came to know each other better, they found they had similar views about Communist domination of Eastern Europe, and quietly worked together to support the Solidarity movement, which eventually led to Poland becoming a free nation.

Poland was not the only nation that benefited from President Reagan's steadfast advocacy for democracy. While he was in the White House, free, democratic elections were held for the first time in many years in the Republic of Korea, Brazil, Argentina, Uruguay, Bolivia, Guatemala, El Salvador, Honduras, and the Philippines. By the time President Reagan left office, the number of people in Latin America living under freely elected governments had tripled from what it had been just ten years earlier.

Championing freedom and standing up to threats against it was more than just a catchphrase for the Reagan administration. In 1983, when he was asked by the Organisation of Eastern Caribbean States, President Reagan sent U.S. troops to Grenada to lead a multinational force in liberating that country from an oppressive Marxist dictatorship. Not only were the Communists ousted, the troops also rescued nearly one thousand American medical students whose safety had been in jeopardy under the brutal regime.

Growing up in the heartland of America taught Ronald Reagan the importance of being a good neighbor. As president, he paid special attention to our neighbors to the north and south—Canada and Mexico. Wasting no time in reaching out, he took the unprecedented step of visiting Mexico as president-elect, and visited six more times while in the White House. He made Canada the first foreign country he visited as president, traveling there less than two months after assuming office, the first of five trips. While President Reagan enjoyed strong relationships with all of the Mexican and Canadian leaders during his presidency, Prime Minister Brian Mulroney of Canada became a particularly staunch ally and valued personal friend.

Over his eight years as president, there were some frustrations in foreign policy, chief among which was the elusiveness of lasting peace in the Middle East. Progress was made, such as the finalization of the Israeli–Egyptian peace treaty, but the region remained unstable—as it had been for centuries. The 1983 bombing of U.S. Marine Corps barracks in Beirut, Lebanon, was particularly sad. Perhaps the greatest disappointment of the administration's foreign policy, it was by no means its defining event.

In sharp contrast to Beirut, President Reagan's spectacular achievement of redefining the U.S.–Soviet relations would have a lasting, positive effect on both nations. This massive shift in relations did not happen by accident. President Reagan came into office with a specific plan for change. The United States would no longer let the Soviets get away with the aggressive exportation of repressive policies. Not only that, but President Reagan also intended to reduce the number of nuclear weapons on both sides.

In speaking of that, President Reagan would often say, "We don't mistrust each other because we're armed; we're armed because we mistrust each other." He believed that if the mistrust was eliminated, then so, too, could be the dangerous weapons. President Reagan was confident that if he could just get his Soviet counterpart in a room and tell him face-to-face that America had no hostile intent, the mistrust would evaporate. Instinctively he knew that could not be accomplished through the traditional diplomacy of a bureaucratic State Department. So, to the horror of some longtime career government employees, he did what no president had ever done. While still recovering from the assassination attempt in 1981, he handwrote a letter to Soviet leader Leonid Brezhnev, seeking to find common ground and establish a better tone for relations between the White House and the Kremlin. As things turned out, the president would have to be patient—very patient. Brezhnev died in November 1982, and was replaced by Yuri Andropov.

Our defense policy is based on a very
simple premise: The United States
will not start fights. We will not be
the first to use aggression. We will
not seek to occupy other lands
or control other peoples. Our strategy
is defensive; our aim is to protect the
peace by ensuring that no adversaries
ever conclude they could best us
in a war of their own choosing.

―――――――

Ronald Reagan,
statement on United States
Defense Policy, March 9, 1983

Less than two years later, Andropov died, and was succeeded by Konstantin Chernenko. Incredibly, Chernenko died just thirteen months later. "They kept dying on me," President Reagan said, expressing frustration at the difficulty in establishing a dialogue with the Kremlin chief. Perhaps realizing the risks of anointing elderly men, after Chernenko died the Soviet high command chose a younger leader, Mikhail Gorbachev, to take charge.

It was Gorbachev with whom President Reagan would finally have that long-sought opportunity to form a new relationship, one that would lead to a lessening of tensions between Washington and Moscow and eventually to meaningful arms reduction.

The first of their five meetings was on neutral turf. It took place in Geneva, Switzerland, in November 1985. There, in a small, plain boathouse just down a stone path from Fleur d'Eau, the grand château where their formal sessions took place, President Reagan and General Secretary Gorbachev sat down in two comfortable chairs in front of a roaring fireplace. With only interpreters present, the two men began to forge a relationship that would not only improve U.S.–Soviet relations, but would turn out to be the beginning of the end not only of Soviet domination of Eastern Europe but, ultimately, of the Soviet Union itself.

Almost a year later, the two leaders met again, this time in Reykjavik, Iceland. In a summit meeting not long in the making, they met at Hofdi House, a picturesque waterfront structure that once housed the French consulate. There they came tantalizingly close to an agreement to eliminate all medium-range missiles based in Europe. At the last minute, Gorbachev insisted that the United States abandon plans for a space-based missile defense system. Despite President Reagan's offer to share the system's technology with the Soviet Union so that both countries could be protected, Gorbachev dug in his heels and would not budge. The last thing Ronald Reagan would ever do would be to risk America's safety for the sake of an agreement. The summit was over. Anger, sadness, and deep disappointment were etched in President Reagan's face as he emerged from Hofdi House. There was chatter that this was the end of the Reagan–Gorbachev relationship, and

that there would be no more summits. President Reagan knew better. Partly because of his natural optimism, and partly because he believed that Gorbachev shared his desire to make the world safer, he was certain that talks eventually would resume. The president directed his team to keep the dialogue going and to see whether the progress made in Reykjavik could be the basis for successful negotiations going forward. That's exactly what happened.

Having a noteworthy measure of confidence in the strength of his newly established relationship with Gorbachev, but dissatisfied with the token Soviet gestures toward change and openness taken thus far, Reagan traveled to West Berlin and witnessed firsthand the stark contrast between two political systems. On one side, people were held captive by a failed and

President Reagan and General Secretary Gorbachev at the conclusion of their meetings in Reykjavik, Iceland, where the U.S.S.R. refused to compromise on an arms reduction agreement, 1986.

corrupt totalitarian government; on the other side, freedom, enterprise, and prosperity were flourishing. On June 12, 1987, just eight months after Reykjavik, President Reagan stood at the Brandenburg Gate and fearlessly launched a decisive challenge to Gorbachev, "Come here to this gate! Mr. Gorbachev, open this gate! Mr. Gorbachev, tear down this wall!" Though career diplomats were concerned about this bold stance, history has shown that it was not only one of Ronald Reagan's most poignant examples of principled leadership, it was also a significant turning point in the relationship between the United States and the U.S.S.R.

In spite of having publicly challenged Gorbachev in Berlin, President Reagan was certain that Gorbachev was still committed to lessening tensions and establishing lasting peace between their countries, and that he would return to negotiations. As hoped, on December 8, 1987, the two leaders met in the East Room of the White House to sign the historic INF Treaty, eliminating all nuclear-armed ground-launched ballistic and cruise missiles with ranges between 500 and 5,000 kilometers. For the first time ever, the number of nuclear arms was actually being reduced rather than merely limited. The mood was upbeat and celebratory, concluding with a glittering state dinner later that evening in honor of the Gorbachevs.

During the fourth summit in the spring of 1988, Gorbachev and Reagan signed the now-ratified INF Treaty in Moscow. The final summit of the Reagan presidency took place in New York in December 1988, where, in a symbolic handing-off of the official relationship, President-elect George H. W. Bush met with Gorbachev.

The unlikely pairing of a devoted anti-communist with a dyed-in-the-wool Marxist resulted not only in the most significant arms reduction treaty in history, but in a permanent change in U.S.–Soviet relations. Neither country, nor the world, would ever be the same again.

President Reagan delivering his famous "Mr. Gorbachev, Tear Down This Wall" speech at the Brandenburg Gate in West Berlin, Germany, 1987.

After all our struggles
to restore America, to revive
confidence in our country,
hope for our future, after
all our hard-won victories
earned through the patience
and courage of every citizen,
we cannot, must not, and
will not turn back. We will
finish our job. How could we
do less? We're Americans.

———

Ronald Reagan,
State of the Union,
January 25, 1984

President Reagan honoring the men who "stormed the beach" in a worldwide address at Pointe du Hoc in Normandy, France, 1984. **Pages 178–179:** President Reagan addressing the Joint Session of Congress on the State of the Union at the United States Capitol, 1984.

President Reagan working aboard Air Force One, 1984.

President Reagan addressing a large crowd on the tarmac of the
Cedar Rapids, Iowa, airport during his reelection campaign, 1984.

President Reagan at a campaign rally, 1984. **Page 185:** President Reagan campaigning in California, 1984.

Every promise, every
opportunity is still golden
in this land. And through that
golden door our children can
walk into tomorrow with
the knowledge that no one can
be denied the promise
that is America.

———————

Ronald Reagan,
remarks accepting the presidential
nomination at the Republication
National Convention, 1984

President and Mrs. Reagan waving to supporters, 1987.

President Reagan and General Secretary Gorbachev signing the INF Treaty in the East Room, 1987. **Pages 186-187:** President Reagan conducting presidential business from the tack room at Rancho del Cielo, 1985.

An American Hero

Ronald Reagan came to the White House with a clear sense of purpose and direction, based on solid principles, which guided every action he took. Beyond this, he was naturally optimistic, enjoyed life, and believed in the inherent goodness of the American people. He was comfortable with who he was and he genuinely liked people. Those characteristics may not sound like much, but when you're president, they can make all the difference. He inspired Americans to believe in themselves again; it was this jolt of confidence that, coupled with clear policies, addressed the issues at hand that got the country back on track.

President Reagan never tired of meeting people. He was genuinely fond of campaigning, not just because he could advocate for his political positions on key issues, but mostly because he enjoyed being with people. You could see it in his eyes. There was a certain sparkle when he shook hands and engaged in conversation. He wasn't just "going through the motions"; he genuinely listened to what people had to say and thought about what he could do to help. Often, after an event, when he was back in his car or on Air Force One, he would turn to an aide and say, "There was a man back there who . . . " and he would describe the person's plight. Then, either alone or with staff, he would strategize solutions on how to make things right. He believed in making the extra effort if it encouraged positive change and made an impactful difference in someone's life.

It didn't matter to Ronald Reagan whether you were the CEO of a Fortune 500 corporation or the janitor who cleaned the CEO's office at night. Station in life, gender, race, physical appearance, age—he didn't care about any of those qualifiers. What he did care about was people's feelings. Rumor had it that

President Reagan in the East Room of the White House, 1988.

he once delivered a speech that he knew was not his best. The next day, after reading a newspaper article critical of the speech, he told his staff: "They're right. It wasn't a very good speech, but the poor fella who wrote it worked his heart out, and I was worried he would feel bad if I changed it too much."

As great a speaker as he was, and as eloquent as his speeches were, President Reagan was equally happy telling a joke to a small group of people in a social situation. Maybe it was the theatrical part of him that made him feel good about making his audience laugh. He certainly was not afraid to laugh at himself. At the annual White House Correspondents' Dinners, no one enjoyed the comedians more when they poked fun at the president than the president himself.

His ability to smooth the edges in difficult situations— often through the use of humor—turned political adversaries into friends. It was well known that Speaker of the House Tip O'Neill, a Democratic pol from Massachusetts, would say all sorts of things about President Reagan, some of which were mean-spirited. Rather than get angry, President Reagan invented a rule that O'Neill could say whatever he wanted during the working day, but at 6 P.M., the politics would stop and they would be friends. After a day of intense verbal assaults, it was not uncommon to see those two old Irish pols swapping stories and laughing uproariously with one another in the evening.

Other than when Mrs. Reagan faced breast cancer, President Reagan was not a worrier. He did not need the presidency to feel good about himself or to vanquish deep-seated doubts. He never pretended to be someone other than who he was. He did not adopt a persona to fit the job. He rarely raised his voice or gave in to anger. He could get annoyed from time to time, but it was usually because he was behind schedule and people were kept waiting or otherwise inconvenienced as a result.

One day, for example, he was running late for a haircutting appointment and grumbled about the delay to an aide. The aide told the president not to worry because the barber would wait. In a firm voice, the president explained that was not the point. The point was that his delay caused a delay for everyone else waiting at the barber's shop. From then on, the appointments secretary made certain there were no meetings scheduled immediately prior to President Reagan's appointments with the barber.

President Reagan never thought of himself as being better or more important than anyone else. These qualities—his openness, candor, and confidence—resonated with the American people. Even those who did not agree with his policies liked the man. But plenty of people liked his policies, too, as was evident by his landslide reelection to a second term in 1984.

Despite his popularity, President Reagan never let his ego get in the way of his work. The president understood that life wasn't always about him. On his desk in the Oval Office, President Reagan kept a small plaque with the words: "There is no limit to what a man can do or where he can go if he does not mind who gets the credit." That motto directed everything he did. Next to that plaque was another one that read: "It CAN Be Done"—a not-so subtle reminder to both himself and visitors that, in America, anything is possible.

Those two plaques were still on his desk when President Reagan came to the Oval Office January 20, 1989, the last day of his presidency. As usual, his national security advisor briefed him on overnight developments. The briefing on that particular day was short. Colin Powell told the outgoing president that the world was "quiet" that day. After a few minutes reviewing papers, it was time to leave. He and Mrs. Reagan were to welcome the incoming president and vice president for the traditional pre-inauguration coffee. As he walked out the door, he looked back over his shoulder at what had been his office for almost three thousand days. He smiled and waved to the photographers gathered to capture "the final moment."

He was in good spirits as he and Mrs. Reagan hosted the Bushes, Quayles, and senior congressional leaders in the Blue Room. Reagan reported that he was proud of what had been accomplished while he was "custodian" of the presidency and that he was looking forward to the next chapter of his life.

As Ronald Reagan walked out of the White House for the last time as president, an aide standing at the far end of the room looked at the fortieth president and, with tears in his eyes, quietly said, "There will never be another one like him."

Top: President Reagan swapping Irish jokes with House Speaker Thomas "Tip" O'Neill, 1983. **Bottom:** President and Mrs. Reagan taking part in the nation's birthday celebration by visiting New York Harbor for the International Naval Review, 1986.

Top: President Reagan walking from the Oval Office with Israeli Prime Minister Shimon Peres, 1986. **Bottom:** President and Mrs. Reagan congratulating Kennedy Center honorees in the Green Room, 1986. **Page 196:** President Reagan working in his Residence office, 1987.

And come January, when I saddle
up and ride into the sunset it will
be with the knowledge that we've
done great things. We kept faith
with a promise as old as this land
we love and as big as the sky.
A brilliant vision of America as a
shining city on a hill.... America's
greatest chapter is still to be
written, for the best is yet to come.

———

Ronald Reagan,
at a dinner honoring Representative
Jack F. Kemp of New York,
December 1, 1988

President Reagan riding his horse at Camp David, 1986. **Opposite, top:** President Reagan at his surprise birthday party in the Old Executive Office Building, 1987. **Opposite, middle:** Aboard Air Force One, President Reagan gives "orders of the day" to his sleeping Chief of Staff Howard Baker, 1987. **Opposite, bottom:** President Reagan, flanked by Secretary of State George Shultz and Secretary of Defense Caspar Weinberger, during a meeting in the Cabinet Room, 1987.

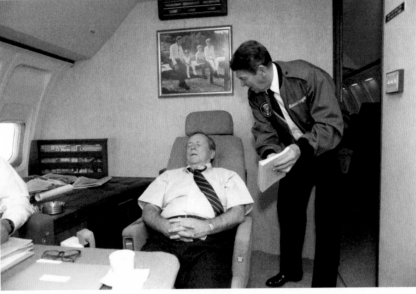

President Reagan talking with Pope John Paul II in Miami, 1987.
Opposite: President Reagan and Pope John Paul II strolling through the gardens of Florida's Vizcaya Museum, 1987.

President Reagan addressing a Joint Session of Congress on the State of the Union. He is holding just a portion of the national budget, about which he said, "Congress shouldn't send another one of these . . . I will not sign it," 1988.

President Reagan listening to a national security briefing in the Oval Office, 1988. **Page 205:** President Reagan and Vice President Bush walking along the colonnade outside the Oval Office, 1988.

When it comes to the economy,
there are two big facts to keep in mind.
Before we came to Washington,
our economy was in a mess: Inflation
in double digits, men and women being
thrown out of jobs, the prime interest
rate soaring at the highest level since
the Civil War. And the second big fact—
well, the second big fact is that when
our administration had put its economic
program in place, the economy stopped
shrinking and started to grow,
and it's been growing ever since.

———

Ronald Reagan,
radio address to the nation
on the economy, July 16, 1988

Top: President Reagan and Vice President George Bush in the Oval Office, 1988. **Bottom:** President Reagan participating in the annual "class photo" at the G-7 Economic Summit in Toronto. From left to right: Jacques Delors, Ciriaco de Mita, Prime Minister Margaret Thatcher, President Reagan, Brian Mulroney, François Mitterrand, Helmut Kohl, and Noboru Takeshita, 1988. **Opposite:** President Reagan following his address at the Republican National Convention in New Orleans, where he asked the enthusiastic crowd to "win just one for the Gipper," 1988.

President-elect Bush, President Reagan, and General Secretary Gorbachev standing outside, during a meeting at Governors Island, 1988. **Opposite:** President Reagan touring Red Square with General Secretary Gorbachev during the Moscow Summit, 1988.

President Reagan riding in a wagon during a Bush–Quayle
Victory '88 Rally in Mesquite, Texas.

President Reagan waving to the White House staff, who gathered in the Rose Garden the day after the presidential election, 1988.
Page 212: President Reagan saluting the troops and the nation as he boards Marine One with Mrs. Reagan at the U.S. Capitol following the inaugural ceremonies, 1989.

It's been the honor of my life
to be your president. So many
of you have written the past few
weeks to say thanks, but I could
say as much for you. Nancy and I
are grateful for the opportunity
you gave us to serve.

———

Ronald Reagan,
Farewell Address to the Nation,
January 11, 1989

Chapter Five

THE LEGEND

Beyond
the White House

There were no hard and fast rules about what a former president should or should not do when Ronald Reagan prepared to leave office. The American political system did not have an established set of expectations for ex–chief executives. It was standard procedure for former presidents to write autobiographies, establish presidential libraries, and perhaps politick for party candidates. Beyond that, however, the role of a former president largely depended on how he shaped it. Although Reagan was proud to have been elected president twice, and was aware of the fact that those accomplishments made him more famous than anything else he had done, he did not view his service as president as the only important chapter of his life. There had been other moments in his life—his time spent at Eureka College, WHO Radio, and Warner Bros. and as the governor of California—that meant something to him, too. Reagan did not view leaving the White House as the end of anything, but rather as the start of an exciting and meaningful new chapter in his life that would be active and fulfilling. He was in the unique position

One of many official presidential portraits, 1980s.

of leaving office after two successful terms as president—the first president to do so since Dwight D. Eisenhower. And he remained immensely popular. Whether or not he wanted to be in the public eye, he was certainly in high demand. World leaders valued his insight and friendship, political candidates wanted and needed his help, and the public at large still wanted to know what he thought about key issues.

He was excited about his foundation and building his presidential library and museum. He also was looking forward to writing his autobiography and expressing some thoughts that were probably better shared once he was out of office. Ronald Reagan understood the unique platform a former president could have, and was determined to use it in a way that continued to serve his country and advance the cause of freedom around the world. The remaining years of his life, from 1989 to 2004, were punctuated by several personal and professional milestones, and he proved to be every bit as active as he had been as president.

Portrait of President Reagan in the White House Colonnade, 1980s.

1989

As much as he loved every minute of serving as the country's fortieth president and considered it a great and humbling honor, there was a part of Ronald Reagan that always longed to return to his home state, California. Simply put, he loved it there. The weather was beautiful most of the time. He could visit his ranch whenever he wished. He and Nancy had many friends whom they missed. He often said that California was "not a place, but a way of life."

So when it was time to go back home, President Reagan was ready, even excited. It would not have surprised any of his aides to hear him whistling "California, Here I Come" in his last days in the White House. Other than weekends at Camp David, where he and Nancy could unwind and have some privacy, he would miss the trappings of the presidency very little, if at all. What he would miss were the people—the men and women who had helped him accomplish so much over those eight years. He valued those relationships and was genuinely saddened about saying goodbye to many he considered dear personal friends.

But he had done what he set out to do in Washington, and now it was someone else's turn. Besides, President Reagan had no intention of retiring or fading from the scene. He intended to continue speaking out on issues that mattered most to him—creating a constitutional amendment to require a balanced budget, reforming the process by which congressional districts are drawn, and giving future presidents line-item veto power. He would also speak out in favor of eliminating term limits on the presidency, which he felt was an unfair restriction of the people's ability to choose their leaders. When speaking of that, he was always quick to point out that changes in term limit laws would be of no benefit to him since he was "already out to pasture." And he would take an active role in the building of a Presidential Library and Museum, as well as writing his autobiography. There was much to do.

When his plane touched down at Los Angeles International Airport on January 20, 1989, Ronald Reagan was happy. He was home. He and Nancy had purchased a beautiful but modest home in Los Angeles, he had offices in a gleaming new tower a short drive from their house, and he had brought with him a few trusted aides from the White House to help with the adjustment to "private life" and the next chapter of his public life.

Not surprisingly, there was very little adjusting Ronald Reagan needed to do. Maybe because he came to the presidency at a later stage in his life than most of his predecessors, the office did not define him. He did not need or crave attention or power, nor did he miss it. He did confess that for the first few weeks, he would occasionally stop in his tracks when he heard a television news anchor say, "Today, the president . . ." and wonder what he had done. Other than that, Ronald Reagan easily returned to being a private citizen again.

Life back home settled into a routine. The week began on Sunday mornings with worship services at Bel Air Presbyterian Church, where the Reagans had been members and regular attendees for many years. Much to their dismay, the Reagans had to refrain from attending church services while in the White House because of the elaborate security arrangements required and the inconveniences that it would have posed to other churchgoers. They missed attending church, and were happy to be able to go again. In fact, they showed up at Bel Air Presbyterian the very first Sunday after they returned home.

On most weekdays, Reagan would get up early, put on
a suit and tie, and head to the office. In a major change from
the previous eight years, his car stopped at red lights. Far from
being annoyed at having to sit in Los Angeles's notorious traffic,
Ronald Reagan delighted in waving to startled pedestrians
and people in other cars who happened to notice the nation's
fortieth president waiting for the light to change.

His days in the office generally followed a structure similar
to that in Washington. He would first meet with a few aides to
catch up on the news, review the day's appointments and events,
and make decisions about upcoming travel. Then he would go to
his desk to work on speeches, correspondence, and his book, or he
would receive visitors. There was a steady stream of a wide variety
of callers—everyone from current and former heads of state to
junior-level White House aides who wanted to say hello. All were
welcome, and he never tired of taking visitors to the window to
show the spectacular view his thirty-fourth-floor office afforded.
On clear days, he could see all the way to the Pacific Ocean.

Most days, he had lunch at a small table in his office,
though every so often he would go to a local restaurant with
staff members or a friend. Everywhere he went, patrons stood
and applauded as he entered and exited, which always seemed to
surprise—and delight—him. After lunch it was back to work,
and then home to Nancy.

Once a week, more or less, he would play golf. Since his
schedule was abbreviated, on those days he would come to
the office in a short-sleeved shirt and casual slacks. Visitors
scheduled for that day were told in advance that former
President Reagan would be informally dressed.

Weekends were often spent at the ranch. If his schedule
allowed, he would take Fridays and Mondays off so as to have
a solid four days there. The Reagans did what they had always
done—horseback riding together in the mornings, followed by
chores and general relaxing in the afternoons.

While Los Angeles was his base of operations, it was on
what he called "the mashed potato circuit" that Ronald Reagan
continued to be a political force. In high demand as a speaker, he
spent much of his time on the road, talking to audiences around

the country—college students, charitable and community-service organizations, civic leaders, business groups, and political gatherings. He was happy to be free of the protective bubble of the presidency so he could shake hands, sign autographs, pose for pictures, and just talk to ordinary people again. He especially delighted in taking questions from his audiences on any subject they wanted, telling them, "I'll bet you've said to yourself, 'Boy, if I could ever ask him . . . ' Well, this is your chance." Ask they did—everything from sophisticated questions about major presidential decisions to details about life in the White House. He was warmly received everywhere he went, and loved being back with the people. His audiences clearly felt a connection to the man, and he felt the same toward them.

Even though he crisscrossed the country often, Reagan's visits to the White House were rare. In the fall of 1989, he and Nancy returned for an East Room ceremony at which his official portrait was unveiled. In 1993, he was back in his former residence to receive the Presidential Medal of Freedom.

Reagan's popularity was as high overseas as it was at home. World leaders around the globe invited him to visit

Ronald Reagan leaving the home of U.S. publisher Malcolm Forbes in Battersea, London, 1989.

their countries so they could bestow honors for what he had accomplished. The first trip abroad was to Europe in June 1989. Following a private luncheon at Buckingham Palace, he was made an Honorary Knight Grand Cross Order of the Bath by Queen Elizabeth II—a rare honor for an American president. While in London, he gave the annual Winston Churchill Lecture to the English-Speaking Union. The trip also included a visit to France, where he was inducted as one of only twelve foreign associates into the prestigious Academy of Moral and Political Sciences of the Institute of France in Paris, and was a guest of honor at ceremonies marking the one-hundredth anniversary of the Eiffel Tower.

Soon after returning from Europe, the Reagans traveled to Mexico to spend a few days with friends at a ranch. While there, Reagan, a very experienced rider, was thrown by an unruly horse and sustained injuries that at the time were thought to be only superficial. It would become clear later that that was not the case.

Being out of office allowed Reagan to have a little fun, too. In July 1989, he returned to his sports broadcasting roots by serving in the booth as a guest announcer for an inning of major league baseball's All-Star Game played in Anaheim.

A few weeks later, a routine annual physical examination at the Mayo Clinic in Rochester, Minnesota, revealed that the injuries Reagan had sustained as a result of being bucked by the horse in Mexico were far more serious than originally thought. A subdural hematoma—a collection of blood on the surface of the brain—was discovered. Immediate surgery was required. The Mayo doctors operated successfully, and the former president was no worse for the wear, other than being left with a military-style haircut, which he seemed to like. Mrs. Reagan and staff members did not share his enthusiasm for the new look.

Even while he was recovering from head surgery, Reagan's status as a world leader did not diminish. Soviet politician Boris Yeltsin, traveling in the United States at the time, insisted on coming to visit him in the hospital. Doctors gave permission, and the two had a friendly chat.

1990–1991

A little more than a month after leaving the hospital, the Reagans were headed overseas again, this time to Japan. At the Imperial Palace in Tokyo, the emperor awarded Ronald Reagan the Grand Cordon of the Supreme Order of the Chrysanthemum, and, with the empress, hosted a luncheon in the Reagans' honor. Reagan also met the prime minister and made speeches in Tokyo and Osaka.

The following year brought more high-profile events for the busy former president. In April, he hosted a ceremony at his Presidential Library to receive a piece of the Berlin Wall. A few weeks later, the Reagans and Gorbachevs were together again, this time in San Francisco. Like long-lost friends, the couples greeted each other with broad smiles and bear hugs. The following month, Reagan joined his predecessors and successor in speaking at the dedication of the Richard Nixon Presidential Library. He clearly enjoyed being a member of this unique fraternity.

The rest of the summer featured speeches in a variety of forums, including the opening ceremony at the Goodwill Games in Seattle, Washington, and the rededication of the Dwight D. Eisenhower Presidential Library and Museum in Abilene, Kansas.

In early September of 1990, the Reagans embarked on a ten-
day trip to Europe. First stop, the newly united Germany.
In Berlin, he returned to the Brandenburg Gate, where he had
called for the Berlin Wall to be torn down, and actually took
a chisel to a remaining section. Witnesses described the scene
of Ronald Reagan chipping away at the Berlin Wall as surreal.
Chancellor Helmut Kohl awarded his former colleague the
Grand Cross Order of Merit of the Federal Republic of Germany.
From Germany, the Reagans traveled to Poland, where they
toured the Warsaw Ghetto and the former president addressed
the Polish Parliament. He also met with Lech Walesa and
addressed workers at the shipyard in Gdansk. Many Poles credit
former President Reagan and Pope John Paul II with being
driving forces behind Poland's freedom, and he was welcomed
like a hero. Next stop was Russia. After a brief time in Leningrad,
where they toured the Hermitage Museum, the Reagans went
to Moscow. They were warmly received by the Gorbachevs. The
former president addressed the International Affairs Committee

of the Supreme Soviet and met with Boris Yeltsin, who was now president of the Russian Republic. The final leg of the trip took them to Italy for meetings with the country's president and prime minister, and finally an audience with Pope John Paul II at Castel Gandolfo, outside of Rome.

The rest of the year in Los Angeles brought visits from a host of world leaders, including President Herzog of Israel, Prime Minister Antall of Hungary, and President Zhelev of Bulgaria, among others. In November, Reagan's much-anticipated autobiography, *An American Life*, was published, and the Reagans ended the year with a trip to England, where he addressed students and faculty at Cambridge University.

Nineteen ninety-one started off on a happy note for Reagan, when he and Nancy welcomed former Prime Minister Margaret Thatcher of Britain and her husband, Denis, for a private tour

Ronald Reagan addressing workers at the shipyard in Gdansk, Poland, 1990. **Opposite:** Ronald Reagan visiting Germany, where he eagerly chipped away at a remnant of the Berlin Wall, September 1990.

of his Presidential Library. A few days later, the former president celebrated his eightieth birthday, which he referred to as "the forty-first anniversary of my thirty-ninth birthday."

The rest of the year unfolded much like the previous two. There were visits from a long and impressive list of world leaders, including President Chamorro of Nicaragua, President Walesa of Poland, President Landsbergis of Lithuania, Soviet Foreign Minister Shevardnadze, Prime Minister Rabin of Israel, President Havel of the Czech Republic, Prime Minister Nakasone of Japan, and Mother Teresa. Some were received in the former president's office, some at his home, and some at the Presidential Library. Reagan appreciated and enjoyed the visits, and staying involved. But out of respect for his successor in the Oval Office, even in private meetings, Reagan never offered an opinion that differed on foreign policy issues.

He did, however, publicly differ with President Bush on one important domestic matter—passage of the Brady Bill. In an emotional speech to students and faculty at George Washington University on the tenth anniversary of the assassination attempt on his life, the former president stated his full support for the bill and urged swift congressional approval. He knew that he would face criticism from many in his own party for his position, but he believed it was the right thing to do, and he had given his word to Sarah Brady that he would help. Once Ronald Reagan gave his word, it was as good as done.

In addition to unambiguously stating his support for the Brady Bill, former President Reagan's speech at George Washington University was noteworthy for his poignant words to the students: "My young friends, savor these moments. Keep the memories close to your heart. Cherish your family and friends. As I learned ten years ago, we never really know what the future will bring."

That speech was a high point of the year, but not the only notable one. In early May, former President Reagan returned to his old stomping grounds of Sacramento, California, where he addressed the Joint Legislature. Later in the month, he and Nancy traveled across the country to join Queen Elizabeth II and Prince Philip for dinner aboard the Royal Yacht *Britannia*, which was docked in Miami.

The indisputable highlight of the year was the November 4 dedication of the Ronald Reagan Presidential Library and Museum in Simi Valley, California. At the ceremony, the Reagans hosted an unprecedented gathering of five American presidents and six first ladies. It was one of Ronald Reagan's proudest days, and in giving the library and museum to the American people he said: "My fondest hope is that Americans will travel the road extending forward from the arch of experience, never forgetting our heroic origins, never failing to seek divine guidance as we march boldly and bravely into a future limited only by our capacity to dream."

The final trip of that year was to Mexico City, where former President Reagan met with President Salinas and former President de la Madrid of Mexico, and delivered a speech to Nueva Generación.

The Reagans with Jim Brady, 1991.

Five presidents walking in the courtyard of the Ronald Reagan Presidential Library, 1991. **Opposite, top:** The Reagans visiting with Colin and Alma Powell during a Reagan alumni reception preceding the opening of the Ronald Reagan Presidential Library, 1991. **Opposite, middle:** Five presidents and six first ladies at the Ronald Reagan Library opening. From left to right: Lady Bird Johnson, Jimmy and Rosalynn Carter, Gerald and Betty Ford, Richard and Pat Nixon, Ronald and Nancy Reagan, George and Barbara Bush, 1991. The event was historic in that it was the first time five living presidents had been together in one place. **Opposite, bottom:** Ronald Reagan being greeted by supporters during a Bush–Quayle rally, Orange County, California, 1992.

1992–2000

Nineteen ninety-two was a year of special meaning to the Reagans. On March 4, they celebrated their fortieth wedding anniversary. The year was every bit as busy as the previous year, perhaps even more so. After all, it was an election year and Ronald Reagan's unprecedented popularity had a long line of Republican candidates asking him to campaign with them. One candidate who got a lot of help from the former president was his daughter, Maureen, who ran for Congress from California's thirty-sixth district. Even with her dad out on the campaign trail, Maureen fell short.

The parade of world leaders continued unabated throughout the year. The Reagans hosted a tea at their home for President George H. W. and Barbara Bush in February, and in May, they welcomed Mikhail and Raisa Gorbachev to their ranch. The day after the ranch reunion, in a touching ceremony at the Reagan Library and Museum, former President Reagan presented his dear friend the first Ronald Reagan Freedom Award.

Prime Minister Yasuhiro Nakasone of Japan, Prime Minister Chung of South Korea, and Deputy Defense Minister Netanyahu of Israel also came to visit the fortieth president at various points that year. Some days it seemed that Ronald Reagan had never left office.

The schedule was filled with speeches, as usual, one of which touched the former president in a very special way. In May, he visited his alma mater, Eureka College, where he had lunch with the graduating class and addressed their commencement. The next day, he visited his boyhood hometown of Tampico, Illinois. It would be his last time there.

From Illinois he went to New York, where he and Mikhail Gorbachev attended events surrounding the seventy-fifth anniversary of *Forbes* magazine. The two also toured the New York Stock Exchange together.

In August, Ronald Reagan addressed the Republican National Convention in Houston. That would be his final formal address to the party. He campaigned for President Bush and other Republican candidates throughout the country in September and October.

The year ended with a visit from President-elect Bill Clinton, who came to the former president's office and was given a jar of jelly beans along with some words of friendly advice. By all accounts, the two men got along quite well.

Ronald Reagan awarding former Soviet leader Mikhail Gorbachev the first Ronald Reagan Freedom Award at the Reagan Library, 1992.

In January, President Bush got the new year off to a splendid start for his predecessor by awarding him the Presidential Medal of Freedom. Former British Prime Minister Margaret Thatcher came to Los Angeles as a guest of honor at a gala dinner at the Reagan Presidential Library and Museum on Ronald Reagan's eighty-second birthday. The next day, she had lunch with the Reagans at their ranch.

In April, another dear friend, Prime Minister Brian Mulroney of Canada and his wife, Mila, visited the Reagan Presidential Library and Museum for a luncheon, and that night had dinner with the Reagans at their ranch. Reagan valued the close personal relationships with Thatcher and Mulroney, and it meant a lot to him that they would come to see him.

Ronald Reagan wearing the Medal of Freedom home from the White House award ceremony, 1993.

He continued to make speeches, and was especially pleased to have been chosen as the commencement speaker at the Citadel in Charleston, South Carolina. The rest of the year was largely occupied by greeting a steady stream of visitors to the office and attending a series of events, mostly in the Los Angeles area.

In September, the Reagans traveled to New York, where he received the Intrepid Freedom Award aboard the USS *Intrepid*.

Nineteen ninety-four was the year that changed everything for Ronald and Nancy Reagan. It began on a high note with a trip to Washington in February, where Margaret Thatcher helped celebrate his eighty-third birthday at a large gala dinner.

In April, Richard Nixon died. The Reagans had been friends with him and his wife, Pat, for many years, and their deep sadness at his passing was obvious on both of their faces when they attended his funeral in Yorba Linda. That event would end up being Ronald Reagan's last major public appearance.

Ronald Reagan stayed close to home for most of the rest of the year. He visited his ranch from time to time, played an occasional game of golf, and continued to receive visits from world leaders, including the emperor and empress of Japan and Prince Charles, as well as former aides and political supporters.

He remained as popular as ever, but there was a noticeable decline in public appearances. Things had changed. The pace was definitely slower, quieter.

On November 5, he told the world why. In a handwritten letter to the American people, the nation's fortieth president announced that he had been diagnosed with Alzheimer's disease. Reagan's words touched the hearts of his biggest fans and his staunchest foes.

RONALD REAGAN

Nov. 5, 1994

My Fellow Americans,

I have recently been told that I am one of the millions of Americans who will be afflicted with Alzheimer's Disease.

Upon learning this news, Nancy & I had to decide whether as private citizens we would keep this a private matter or whether we would make this news known in a public way.

In the past Nancy suffered from breast cancer and I had my cancer surgeries. We found through our open disclosures we were able to raise public awareness. We were happy that as a result many more people underwent testing. They were treated in early stages and able to return to normal, healthy lives.

So now, we feel it is important to share it with you. In opening our hearts, we hope this might promote greater awareness of this condition. Perhaps it will encourage a clearer understanding of the individuals and families who are affected by it.

At the moment I feel just fine, I intend to live the remainder of the years God gives me on this earth doing the things I have always done. I will continue to share life's journey with my beloved Nancy and my family. I plan to enjoy the great outdoors and stay in touch with my friends and supporters.

Unfortunately, as Alzheimer's Disease progresses, the family often bears a heavy burden. I only wish there was some way I could spare Nancy from this painful experience. When the time comes I am confident that with your help she will face it with faith and courage.

In closing let me thank you, the American people for giving me the great honor of allowing me to serve as your President. When the Lord calls me home, ~~whenever~~ whenever that may be, I will leave with the greatest love for this country of ours and eternal optimism for its future.

I now begin the journey that will lead me into the sunset of my life. I know that for America there will always be a a bright dawn ahead.

Thank you my friends. May God always bless you.

Sincerely,
Ronald Reagan

The outpouring of support and praise was nothing short of astounding. Such candor from a public figure who was now a private citizen was without precedent. Those who knew the Reagans were not surprised. That had always been their way. Now the world knew what the Reagans and only a handful of family, friends, and close aides had been living with for months.

Because he was still feeling well, Reagan did not immediately fade from public view. His popularity soared. Throughout 1995 and 1996, he continued to see people at his office and home, including former President and Mrs. Bush, Senator Bob Dole, Margaret Thatcher, Spanish Crown Prince Felipe, and the Reverend Billy Graham, among others. It seemed that there was a deluge of requests. He enjoyed being outdoors in the fresh air, and played golf from time to time. He visited his Presidential Library and Museum often, always pausing to take in the

Ronald Reagan signing bookplates at his desk in the library office, 1993.
Opposite: Ronald Reagan waving to children arriving at the Ronald Reagan Presidential Library, 1993.

spectacular view afforded by its hilltop location and to greet its visitors. Sadly, Ronald Reagan's only sibling, Neil, died in 1996, at the age of eighty-eight.

Reagan continued to receive guests and visit his Presidential Library from time to time in the late 1990s. By 2000, he was spending his time primarily at home. He was happy and his eyes lit up whenever Nancy came into the room. In January 2001, at almost ninety years old, he fell and broke his hip. He underwent surgery to repair it and healed quickly. Later that year, Ronald Reagan's daughter, Maureen, died of melanoma at the age of sixty. He was not able to attend her funeral, though Nancy went.

The remaining years were quiet for Ronald Reagan. Though his voice was stilled, his legacy was not. Across the country, schools, courthouses, office buildings, battleships, turnpikes, and other permanent structures were named for him, all as a way of paying tribute to a man who had changed the country and the world. He would have been a little embarrassed by all of the attention, but he also would have enjoyed it. Even the airport in the nation's capital was renamed in honor of the fortieth president.

Perhaps the most prestigious tribute was one bestowed by the United States Congress, which gave Congressional Gold Medals —its highest civilian award—to both Nancy and Ronald Reagan. On May 17, 2002, Mrs. Reagan received the medal, presented by President George W. Bush in a ceremony at the Capitol.

President George H. W. Bush visiting Ronald Reagan, 1992.

Ronald Reagan sharing personal insights with President-elect
Bill Clinton, 1992. **Page 243:** Ronald Reagan working at his post-
presidential office, Los Angeles, 1992.

Some may try and tell us that
this is the end of an era. But what
they overlook is that in America,
every day is a new beginning,
and every sunset is merely the latest
milestone on a voyage that never
ends. For this is the land that has
never become, but is always in the
act of becoming. Emerson was right:
America is the Land of Tomorrow.

Ronald Reagan,
Presidential Medal of Freedom
Ceremony, The White House,
January 13, 1993

Ronald Reagan preparing for a ride in the Goodyear Blimp, Carson, California, 1992.

Ronald Reagan giving Mikhail Gorbachev a tour of Rancho del Cielo, 1992.

2004

By the spring of 2004, Ronald Reagan's health had declined significantly. As his life was nearing its end, Nancy Reagan was where she had been for more than fifty years—at her husband's side, taking care of him. On the morning of June 5, 2004, just as she had done every day for the past several years, she sat next to her husband's bedside, talking softly and keeping him company. His eyes were closed and his breathing had slowed. Just before slipping away, he opened his blue eyes and looked straight at Nancy. She kissed him and told him that was the greatest gift he could have given her. He closed them for the last time and was gone.

From the moment his passing was officially announced, the outpouring of emotion was overwhelming. From every corner of the world—the grandest palaces to the most modest homes—came tributes and tears. It seemed that Ronald Reagan had touched everyone.

His flag-draped casket was first placed in repose at the Ronald Reagan Presidential Library and Museum in Simi Valley, California, where tens of thousands came to pay their respects. Then it was on to Washington. More than one hundred thousand people filed past his casket in the Capitol Rotunda, with thousands more lined up along the funeral route. The state funeral at Washington's National Cathedral on June 11 drew current and former heads of state from around the world, as well as family, friends, former staffers, and even some former political foes. He was eulogized by Margaret Thatcher, Brian

Mulroney, and both then-President George W. Bush and former President George H. W. Bush. Few eyes were dry as a military honor guard escorted their former commander in chief out of the cathedral for his final trip home. Back in California, after a touching sunset service at the Presidential Library and Museum, Ronald Reagan was laid to rest in the burial site he had helped design.

On it was inscribed the words by which he chose to be remembered: "I know in my heart that man is good, that what is right will always eventually triumph, and that there is purpose and worth to each and every life."

Ronald Reagan was not afraid of death. He spoke often of his faith, that there is a better place to which man goes, and told family and friends he was looking forward to that when his time came.

For him, it now had come.

After proceeding down Constitution Avenue, the horse-drawn caisson bearing the casket of former President Reagan completes its journey at the base of the U.S. Capitol steps, 2004.

Former President Ronald Reagan lying in state in the U.S. Capitol Rotunda, 2004. **Opposite, top:** The horse-drawn caisson processional down Constitution Avenue to the Capitol, Washington, D.C., 2004. **Opposite, bottom:** A large crowd watching the funeral procession, Washington, D.C., 2004.

An Enduring Spirit

So what was he really like? Who was this man who evoked such an emotional response in people, most of whom never met him?

Even people who personally knew Ronald Reagan often had difficulty describing him. A devoted husband and loving father. Optimistic but not naive. Articulate but not glib. Intelligent yet guided by common sense. Well-mannered but never pretentious. Friendly but not a pushover. Charismatic but real. Principled but not intransigent. He was all of that and so much more.

Yet somehow, he remains an enigma. There was just something special about him.

No one knew him better or loved him more than Nancy. She said it best: "They broke the mold when they made Ronnie."

Captain James Symonds, commander, USS *Ronald Reagan*, handing the flag that was draped over Ronald Reagan's casket to Mrs. Reagan at the conclusion of the interment ceremony, Ronald Reagan Library, 2004. **Page 252:** Ronald Reagan's final resting place at the Reagan Library, Simi Valley, California.

I know in my heart that
man is good, that what is
right will always eventually
triumph, and that there
is purpose and worth
to each and every life.

———

Ronald Reagan,
inscription on his memorial site

Ronald Reagan
Presidential Foundation

As the fortieth president of the United States, Ronald Wilson Reagan (1911–2004) not only inspired freedom, but he also changed the world. In 2011, America will commemorate the centennial of Ronald Reagan's 1911 birth with a historic year-long series of activities, events, educational programs, and special projects throughout the United States and abroad. As President Reagan would have wanted, no taxpayer dollars have been apportioned for this occasion. All activities will be funded completely through private donations raised by the Ronald Reagan Presidential Foundation—www.reaganfoundation.org—the sole nonprofit, nonpartisan organization founded by President Reagan to preserve and promote his legacy. The Foundation sustains the Ronald Reagan Presidential Library and Museum, the Reagan Center for Public Affairs, the Walter and Leonore Annenberg Presidential Learning Center, The Air Force One Pavilion, and the award-winning Air Force One Discovery Center. Located in Simi Valley, California, the Library houses sixty-three million pages of gubernatorial, presidential, and personal papers, and over sixty thousand gifts and artifacts chronicling the lives of Ronald and Nancy Reagan. It is one of the most visited presidential libraries in America and now serves as the final resting place of America's fortieth president.

Photography Credits

Art Foto Shop, Bloomington, IL: 28

Geri Bauer: 66

Department of the U.S. Air Force/Air Force Museum: 61

Michael Evans: 104, 107–108

General Electric: 78, 79 (top)

Getty Images: 23 (top), 38, 71, 124, 142–143, 157 (top), 183, 185, 188, 223

Mister D Studio, Nikola Drakulich: 116 (top)

The Reagan family: 14, 17, 19, 20, 23 (bottom), 24, 26, 31, 33, 34, 42 (top), 43, 58, 60, 62–63, 65, 69, 75, 77, 80–81, 85, 88, 91, 92–93, 94–95, 99, 100, 111, 112–113, 115, 117, 119, 120–121, 129, 130, 216, 236–237

Robert C. Ferguson Photography: 74

The Ronald Reagan Presidential Foundation: 209, 229, 238–245, 247, 248–249, 251, 252, 253–254

The Ronald Reagan Presidential Library: 82, 96, 114, 131, 134, 137, 140–141, 144–145, 146–147, 148–149, 150, 152, 154–155, 156, 157 (bottom), 158–159, 160, 164–165, 166–167, 168–169, 172, 175, 177, 180–181, 182, 186–187, 189, 190–191, 194 (bottom), 195, 196, 198–199, 200–208, 210–211, 212, 226–227, 230–231, 233, 234

Warner Bros. Studios: 41, 48, 51, 55, 57, 76, 79 (bottom)

D.H. Zeiger—Eureka, IL: 42 (bottom)

All quotes and speeches by Ronald Reagan printed with permission of the Ronald Reagan Presidential Foundation.